Customer Understanding:
Three Ways to Put the "Customer" in *Customer* Experience (and at the Heart of Your Business)

Annette Franz, CCXP

DEDICATION

If you ever told me I couldn't—well, I could. And I did.

CONTENTS

ACKNOWLEDGMENTS

For those who led the way and inspired me to write this book—the list is endless—thank you. For those who encouraged me to write this book, well, that list is pretty long too. You know who you are, and I appreciate the gentle nudges and the support to keep moving forward.

Annette Franz

FOREWORD

In the golden age of advertising, businesses of all sizes relied on ads to promote and sell their products. Giant corporations used TV commercials and full-page newspaper ads to reach us. Small businesses got our attention by placing ads in the local newspaper. In the past, advertising allowed average products to gain traction. But now, discerning consumers ad-block and ignore.

When conventional advertising became less effective, many businesses migrated to social media platforms. The promise of the digital age was that targeted promotion would enable us to reach more customers for close to free. While it's easier to target and reach prospective customers, there is no guarantee that more people will be won over. That doesn't stop us from spending the majority of our resources trying to reach potential customers—and relatively few to retain existing customers. According to Econsultancy, for every $92 we allocate to creating awareness, we spend $1 on converting the customer.

How can we invest our resources more wisely?

It's difficult to succeed as a business today by trying to make people want things. Making things people already want and need is a far better strategy. Lasting success isn't built around launching one PR campaign after another. It's powered by understanding what people want, giving them a better experience, and exceeding their expectations.

No business can survive, let alone thrive, unless the following four things happen:

- The customers' unmet needs are recognized and satisfied.
- The customers' unspoken desires are understood and met.
- The company tells true stories that align to their customers' worldview.
- The customers want to buy into and share those stories.

Whenever you see a business that's endured, look for the ways that company put their customers at the center of everything they do.

Most companies are focused on growth. We want more leads, more fans, readers, or subscribers who will grow our customer base, resulting in more sales and increased profits. Our plan to get them usually involves targeting tomorrow's potential and unknown customers. We sometimes forget that we find tomorrow's customers by understanding the needs of the customers we have today.

No twenty-first-century business or brand can thrive without understanding what it is their customer wants. No leader can create meaningful change without seeing the world through the eyes of her colleagues. No innovator can create relevant solutions unless he understands the challenge his invention helps someone overcome.

Whether you're an artist or an app developer, a bank or a bakery—it's only possible to make things people love by figuring out the problems you can solve for those people. The first rule of innovation, sales, and marketing is to understand the customer's pain points, often before the customer knows them, and then show her what life will be like in the presence of your product or service.

We have more—big and small, hard and soft—customer data

than ever before. Leveraging it to truly serve and stay relevant to those customers is the greatest business development opportunity there is. Business works best when it's in the service of the customer. Whoever gets closest to their customer wins.

Bernadette Jiwa
Brand Story Strategist & Bestselling Author
https://thestoryoftelling.com/

ENDNOTES
  Econsultancy, "Why are Conversion Rates So Low," https://econsultancy.com/why-are-conversion-rates-so-low-infographic/

Annette Franz

1 INTRODUCTION

I recently attended a webinar about how to develop a customer-centric culture. The webinar was solid, and the presenter did a great job of outlining the foundational elements needed to do just that. As webinars go, there was a Q&A segment at the end, and one of the questions asked was something along the lines of, "But if I focus on the customer, won't that take away from my focus on the product?"

I happened to have just taken a sip of my coffee, and I think it came out of my nose. I cleaned up the coffee and held my breath in hopes that the presenter would answer the question the way it should be answered. She did.

And yet, at the same time, I'm shocked that someone would ask that question. (Okay, only mildly shocked, given the challenges that we customer experience professionals have, but just pretend I was shocked. It makes for a better story.)

Here's the real question: isn't it all the same stuff?

Money is being spent by businesses every day to make changes or improvements, and yet they don't factor in the needs and perspectives of the customer? Weird, no?

Listen. It's all about customer focus. It's all about the customer. It's all about the customer experience. (And that means it's all about the employee more first, but that's for another book.) If you're designing a product without focusing on the customer—without understanding her needs, her pain points, her problems to solve, and jobs to be done—forget it. The product will die. Maybe not tomorrow, but it will die eventually.

In a world where products and services are becoming more and more commoditized, customer experience is the only true differentiator. That means that brands need to fight to stay relevant—yet they truly struggle to not get Blockbuster'd.

Jim Keyes, CEO of Blockbuster, stated in 2008 in a *Motley Fool* interview: *"Neither Redbox nor Netflix are even on the radar screen in terms of competition."* He was more focused on Wal-Mart and Apple and laughed in the face of the disruption that was happening in his own industry. Blockbuster filed for bankruptcy in 2010. Today, Netflix is worth $142 billion (2019), although they are in the midst of their own competitive struggles at the moment.

Jonathan Salem Baskin, a former Blockbuster executive, wrote in *Forbes* that Blockbuster was trying to reimagine itself as a convenience store. Clearly not a sound strategy or one that its customers were aligned with. He wrote:

> *The problem with this strategy is that it never acknowledged, let alone addressed, the fundamental promise and peril of the business: If people didn't come to find movies they wish they hadn't missed in the theaters, no amount of add-on retailing could replace that once-glorious rental income. Blockbuster didn't have a technology problem—digital distribution was minimal, albeit talked about incessantly—but rather a customer problem. It gave them no reason to visit stores in lieu of a latest, greatest hit.*

Okay, this book isn't about Blockbuster, but I'm doing what good customer experience (CX) professionals do: building the business case. There are plenty of examples of companies not putting the "customer" in *customer* experience. Again, it's all customer experience. But if you make decisions, define strategies, develop products or services, design websites, etc., and you don't include the customer in any of that work, you will fail. Customers have choices. They will go elsewhere. They will buy from companies who put the customer in customer experience.

Is your company guilty of not putting the customer in customer experience? Or in the business at all?

I imagine the answer to that question is "Yes." Don't worry. You're not alone. I could cite a ton of examples, and I'll provide more throughout the book because I want to help you build your business case too.

Life's too short to build something nobody wants. –Ash Maurya

ENDNOTES
Source for Blockbuster'd:
https://www.cbinsights.com/research/ouch-getting-blockbusterd/

Source for Motley Fool interview quote:
https://www.fool.com/investing/general/2008/12/10/blockbuster-ceo-has-answers.aspx

Source for Jonathan Salem Baskin quote:
https://www.forbes.com/sites/jonathansalembaskin/2013/11/08/the-internet-didnt-kill-blockbuster-the-company-did-it-to-itself/#4833e7636488

Annette Franz

BUILDING THE BUSINESS CASE

Annette Franz

2 WHAT IS CUSTOMER EXPERIENCE?

Why do I need to define customer experience (CX)? Because if I'm telling you that you need to put the "customer" in customer experience, you have to first know what customer experience is.

There are a lot of definitions of customer experience, but here's the one I like to use:

> *Customer experience is the sum of all the interactions that a customer has with an organization over the life of the "relationship" with that company—and especially or importantly, the feelings, emotions, and perceptions the customer has about those interactions.*

I need to make an important distinction here. A lot of people think "customer experience" and "customer service" are the same thing, when in reality, customer service is just one of those interactions mentioned in the definition.

If you're ever confused about the two, think of it the way that Chris Zane at Zane's Cycles talks about it: *"Customer service is what happens when the customer experience breaks down."*

Think about this: If you got everything else right, perhaps the customer wouldn't need to call customer service. The experience (the "everything else") starts long before the service event. Keep in mind, too, that not every customer's experience even includes a service event.

Another way to look at the difference? Customer experience is proactive, while customer service is reactive. Customer experience is proactive because you intentionally build or design the experience that you want your customers to have—and that they want to have. (Hopefully that means it's based on customer understanding—you understand who they are and what they are trying to achieve, which guides customer experience design.) Customer service is reactive in the sense that you're constantly responding to issues and needs as they arise. It's a bit like Whack-a-Mole, while customer experience is more like Monopoly. A sprint versus a marathon. A point in time versus a lifetime.

Another approach: customer experience is what the customer *feels*; customer service is what the company *does* (for the customer).

And one more: customer service is a department, while customer experience is not; it's a discipline.

And finally, another consideration that really is the main reason you need to differentiate the two: think about the difference as a journey versus a touchpoint. Customer experience is a journey of a thousand (or more) touchpoints; customer service is a touchpoint. Why is this perspective important? When you focus on the entire journey, not solely on individual touchpoints, you deliver a much better experience overall for the customer—and, as a result, for the business. When you just consider touchpoints and single interactions, you're focusing on transactional relationships, not on trusted, long-lasting relationships.

Trust me. When you focus on the customer experience, you're also striving for better customer service. When you design an experience with the customer in mind, you also take some of the pressure off of customer service.

Why customer experience? Why focus on the customer?

Let's think about this for a minute. What's the purpose of a business? The old management adage that companies are in business to maximize shareholder value is the mantra of yesteryear. Yes, companies have to make money, but maximizing shareholder value is an outcome, not the purpose.

So why are you in business? Peter Drucker said: *"There is only one valid definition of business purpose: to create and to nurture a customer."* Amen.

"It is, of course, not possible to state with any practical exactitude what the customer is. But there are several common denominators to be found when we consider the customer in terms of what he is not. These things, I think, are fundamental to intelligent customer relationship, and it may be added, most of them apply pretty well to the vast majority of prospects, as well.

1. The customer is not dependent upon us—we are dependent upon him.

2. The customer is not an interruption of our work—he is the purpose of it.

3. The customer is not a rank outsider to our business—he is a part of it.

4. The customer is not a statistic—he is a flesh-and-blood human being completely equipped with biases, prejudices, emotions, pulse, blood chemistry, and possibly, a deficiency of certain vitamins.

5. The customer is not someone to argue with or match wits against—he is a person who brings us his wants. If we have sufficient imagination, we will endeavor to handle them profitably to him and to ourselves."

Source: 1941 May 2, *Printers' Ink: A Journal for Advertisers, Complaints as an Asset*: [Based on an Interview by P. H. Erbes, Jr., with Kenneth B. Elliott, Vice-president in Charge of Sales, The Studebaker Corporation], Printers' Ink Publishing Company, New York.

The quote from Kenneth Elliott, which is often misattributed to Mahatma Gandhi, on the previous page is a powerful one. That thinking was around in 1941! How did it get lost over the years?

If you focus on creating and, especially, on nurturing customers, shareholders will realize value.

But you can't do that if you're not focused on the customer and on infusing the customer into everything that you do! What are you doing? What are these "competing priorities" that I keep hearing about? Why are you doing the things you're doing for your business if it's not for—and in the best interest of—the customer?

This (customer experience) is not about creating more work or adding more to your plate. It's about doing the things you already do—enhancing the product, changing processes, updating the website, revising policies, hiring new people, etc.—but with a shifted mindset. All I ask is that while you're doing your day job, you think about your customers and how they would feel about what you're producing, the impact of what you're doing or creating on your customers, how customers would feel about changes you want to make, etc.

That's not so hard, is it?

Instead, there's pushback that it takes too much time or that there's no budget for customer experience. What?! How does that even happen?! Again, it's all customer experience. It's all about the customer.

A quick sidebar here: the processes I'll outline in this book are about customer experience, but take the word "customer" and replace it with "employee," and it all applies. Define "customer" as internal or external—however you choose to think of it.

Another sidebar: the employee experience drives the customer experience. Have no doubt about that. Quite simply, without employees, you have no customer experience. Without a great employee experience, you cannot have a great customer experience. Don't forget that.

So let's go back to the question: why customer experience? As Sam Walton said: *"There is only one boss: the customer."* She pays your bills! She keeps your lights on!

As I've already mentioned, in this world where products and services are becoming more and more commoditized every day, customer experience is really *the* one true differentiator. We know that customers are willing to pay more for a better experience, so price can no longer be that differentiator.

PwC recently did some research that showed customers will pay up to a 16 percent premium on products and services. The percentages varied, of course, but do you want to take a stab at which product garnered a 16 percent premium? Coffee. Thank you, Starbucks.

The bottom line is that the experience must be designed right, and the only way to do that is to make sure you bring the customer into that design process.

More companies are starting to understand that they need to focus on customer experience, but many—most—are still struggling. They need help, in many ways. There's a lot of work to be done, and it's certainly not straightforward.

The more we talk about and educate folks on customer experience and help them understand what customer experience is, what's good and what's bad, what's right and what's wrong, the foundational elements that need to be in place to design and deliver a great experience, the better off we will all be.

But, we have a problem . . .

Do companies really put customers at the core of all they do? Are companies really customer-centric?

In short—and, in general—no.

Yes, there are the usual examples of companies who are customer-centric, even customer-obsessed: Amazon, The Ritz

Carlton, Zappos, Southwest Airlines, Warby Parker, Disney, Five Guys, In-N-Out Burger, Ace Hardware, among a few others. Unfortunately, that's not the norm. And there are entire industries that are ripe for customer experience disruption!

What's going on here? More on that in the next chapter.

I constantly remind our employees to be afraid, to wake up every morning terrified. Not of our competition but of our customers. Our customers have made our business what it is, they are the ones with whom we have a relationship, and they are the ones to whom we owe a great obligation. And we consider them to be loyal to us—right up until the second that someone else offers them a better service. -Jeff Bezos

ENDNOTES
Source for PwC research: https://buff.ly/2FzLisr

3 HOUSTON, WE HAVE A PROBLEM

If you're a customer of any business on this planet, no surprise here, you know this: most companies are not really focusing on the customer and the customer experience. They might be giving it lip service—and many are—but that's not the same as actually understanding the customer and designing a great customer experience.

So what's the reality instead? Let me take you through several problems that I'm seeing.

Problem #1: The CX Perception Gap

There are a lot of stats that prove that companies need to be customer-focused, customer-centric . . . even customer-obsessed. My favorite—and the one that proves it best, perhaps!—is the one I refer to as a "CX perception gap." According to 2005 research done by Bain, who refers to this as the "delivery gap:"

- 95% of companies say they are customer-focused
- 80% of executives believe they deliver a "superior experience"
- But only 8% of customers agree

It's a huge gap, and it's concerning. While this research is from 2005, sadly, it's still fairly representative of what's happening today.

Others have done similar research, and the numbers may have moved down and up a bit respectively, but the gap still exists. And the importance of this study lies in the reasons for the gap.

Why does the gap exist? Bain cited two key reasons:

They referred to the first reason as "a business paradox," where companies' growth initiatives hurt their main source of sustainable growth: existing loyal, profitable customers. They do so by trying to suck more revenue out of each customer by doing stupid little things like charging higher transaction fees, hidden fees, etc. On top of that, they focus on acquisition over retention, misdirecting their attention away from their current customer base.

Make no mistake. Both acquisition and retention are important—and both are enterprise-wide efforts. Marketing is the focal area here because acquisition is a marketing function supported by the rest of the organization. Oftentimes, retention dollars—in the form of loyalty programs and customer experience improvement initiatives, etc.—also come from the marketing budget.

In a study by Sitecore and Forbes Insights, the top marketing priority for 58 percent of respondents was attracting new customers; 40 percent cited their top priority as turning current customers into customers for life. In similar research published recently by other sources, the balance is roughly the same.

Why does this dilemma or imbalance exist? Why do marketers focus on acquisition over retention? First, it's easy. It's easier to acquire than to retain; retention is a lot of work. Second, and probably more importantly, growth. Why growth? Where does that reasoning come from? The old management adage that "companies are in business to maximize shareholder value" oftentimes drives this thinking.

Without a doubt, companies need to grow; but when that growth is driven by erroneous thinking, then it's tainted. Clearly, in order to grow, companies must bring in new customers (that they'll then need to retain going forward). The fastest way to grow, and the quickest way to boost short-term revenue, is to win more customers. In addition, focusing on acquisition solves another "problem" that can be a little messier with retention: the return on investment (ROI) is fast and measurable, and CEOs love to report to their shareholders that the business is thriving because their customer base grew by X percent.

The problem, though, is that acquisition costs get more expensive as retention numbers decline. Companies must acquire more customers to fill that leaky bucket. Without customers to retain, acquisition costs continue to increase. Brands can really only fix the retention problem by focusing on delivering the best customer experience. And when that happens, acquisition costs can go down because existing customers will help drive acquisition through word-of-mouth referrals.

Growth gives a false sense of security and of a "superior customer experience." The thought process looks like this: *"We added ten thousand new customers last month. Our experience must be great for all these new customers to come to us!"*

The second reason cited by Bain for the gap is that good relationships are hard to build; it's challenging for businesses to keep promises made and to maintain a dialogue with customers that allows companies to adapt products and services to their changing needs. Bain believes that customer understanding efforts backfire because companies focus more on collecting and analyzing data ad nauseam, as well as on metrics, than on doing what it takes to improve the experience.

No argument there. That totally aligns with what I've been saying and writing about for years. In order to transform the customer experience, it's critical that you listen to your customers. Unfortunately, customer listening has two major flaws—or more accurately, companies have two major shortcomings when it comes to customer listening.

The first shortcoming is: **lack of action**. You've got tons of feedback, tons of data, and you do nothing with it. What a shame! You really are just "collecting" feedback like you collect stamps, as I like to say.

Have you ever collected stamps or know someone who does? You go to the post office, buy sheets of the desired stamp, bring them home, put them in a stamp collector book, put the book on the shelf, and never look at it again.

The same things happens when companies listen to customers: they simply collect feedback and then do nothing with it.

There's an old Gartner statistic that personifies this well, and I still like to share it because I believe it's relevant to this day:

Ninety-five percent of companies collect customer feedback, yet only 10 percent use the feedback to improve, and only 5 percent tell customers what they are doing in response to what they heard.

Like those stamps, the data sits on the proverbial shelf and ages and gets dusty.

Stop the madness! Your customers have given you their precious time to tell you what you're doing right and what you're doing wrong. They're trying to help you. And yet, you waste that feedback by doing nothing with it. It becomes worthless.

Why? Here are some of the issues that lead to inaction. You:

- Don't know where to start; you know you're supposed to listen but don't know where to go from there.
- Haven't outlined clear objectives for your listening efforts.
- Haven't engaged with stakeholders to find out what they'd like to learn from customers.
- Haven't asked questions in a way that they are actionable.
- Haven't asked the right questions, so the data itself isn't even actionable; specific improvements aren't apparent.
- Haven't assigned owners to questions to ensure you know who's accountable for each feedback item.
- Haven't asked any open-ended questions, which can/will add rich commentary and insights to help you hone in on

specific issues or identify emerging trends.

- Don't analyze the feedback/data.
- Don't know how to analyze the feedback to tease out the story, the actions to be taken.
- Analyze the data but don't link it with existing operational, transactional, or interactional customer data in your customer resource management (CRM) system, bringing the customer to life and allowing for more customized, personalized improvements.
- Don't know what the analysis means, assuming you analyzed the data, or how to interpret it to make it actionable.
- Don't know how to share the data in a way that it can be acted upon.
- Don't share the data with those who need to act on it.

There are more reasons that customer feedback goes stale and isn't used. I'll leave it at that for now. You get the picture.

Let's move on to the second flaw.

Have you ever heard of Goodhart's Law? It states: *"When a measure becomes a target, it ceases to be a good measure."* Or similarly, *"Any observed statistical regularity will tend to collapse once pressure is placed upon it for control purposes."*

According to Wikipedia, its origin lies in finance and economics:

The original formulation by Goodhart, a former advisor to the Bank of England and Emeritus Professor at the London School of Economics, is this: 'As soon as the government attempts to regulate any particular set of financial assets, these become unreliable as indicators of economic trends.' This is because investors try to anticipate what the effect of the regulation will be, and invest so as to benefit from it.

You probably already know where I'm going from here. The second shortcoming is: **the metric, not the customer, becomes the focus.**

This is a big problem, and quite honestly, it's also one of the issues that should be added to the list of what causes inaction. Companies focus on the metric, on moving the metric, and not on the customer and the customer experience. Listening becomes all about *"How do we rate today?"* And while it's good to gauge your performance, the movement of the metric is an outcome down the line—the first area of focus ought to be: what's going on with the customer experience, and how do you improve it?

So instead, too many executive conversations start with, *"How do we improve the metric?"* rather than, *"How do we improve the experience?"*

A metric is just that, a metric, a way of measuring your progress. If you make it the endpoint, you'll fail at the journey.

If you've ever received a candy bar, a (large) discount off your next purchase, a free oil change, or a free Sam's Club membership (I've been offered all of these), with a plea to, *"Please rate me a 10 out of 10 on the survey you'll get tomorrow, otherwise I'll get fired,"* then you know that business is focused on the metric and not on you and your experience—or the employees, for that matter.

Metrics can help to rally the troops around the customer—but that's only if they're presented in the right context. It's not the right context if you:

- Mention the score without even talking about the customer and the customer experience (yes, this does happen!);
- Game surveys (selecting certain customers, surveying at a specific time when you know scores will be better, offering incentives a la "the car dealer curse," etc.) just to get a score;
- Threaten disciplinary action or lost compensation if an employee doesn't achieve a score, especially if the employee doesn't have a clear line of sight to his impact on the customer experience or understand what the score links to;
- Do tactical things to move the needle rather than think big picture about how to improve the experience.

How can you avoid the metric becoming the target rather than the indicator? Consider these suggestions:

- Talk about customers and what your customers are saying about the company and its products and services.
- Make the metric the last thing you talk about—or don't talk about it at all.
- Tell stories about customer successes and customer pain points.
- Focus on employee behaviors and what it takes to improve the experience.
- Share customer feedback, verbatims, emotions, and what's important to customers.
- Act on the feedback.
- Coach and praise based on feedback and the experience the customer had.
- Focus on customer outcomes first then business outcomes.
- Ensure that employees have a clear line of sight to the customer.
- Give them a clear understanding of how they contribute to the customer experience.
- Build a culture where the customer is at the center of all you do and no decisions are made unless you ask, *"What would the customer think of this?"*

Don't measure for the sake of measuring, and don't listen just for the sake of measuring. Listen because you want to understand the customer and where the experience is falling down (or going well). And then act on what you hear.

The behaviors that drive a focus on the metric are not the behaviors that improve the experience; they only/simply move the needles, giving a false sense of a "superior customer experience." Don't just focus on improving the score; improve the experience, and the numbers will follow.

Wow! That was only Problem #1. But it is a big problem. Let's move on to the others.

Annette Franz

Problem #2: Misplaced Focus

There are a lot of ways that executives can misplace focus—away from the customer. I've already mentioned a couple of examples: the webinar question about product focus without customer focus, the focus on metrics, and the age-old debate about acquisition over retention. (And I'm still trying to identify the "competing priorities" that I mentioned earlier in the book.)

Acquiring customers can be so much easier than retaining; retention is hard work, and it's a huge part of what the customer experience transformation is all about. Focusing on acquisition can yield a much faster return on investment, especially when companies are driven by growth metrics.

Because retention—and hence customer experience transformation—work is slow and difficult, people get bored and tend to fall back into their old habits rather than relentlessly driving toward the ultimate goal. It's important to recognize that a customer experience transformation is all about baby steps. In order to keep people energized and focused, share quick wins and celebrate successes as you progress.

Related to the misplaced focus on acquisition is the message you receive from the CEO that starts with, *"Revenue is down this quarter. We need all hands on deck focusing on drumming up new business."* Suddenly, all of your customer experience transformation resources are shifted to business development and sales efforts.

Interestingly enough, the first question the CEO should ask is: *"Why are sales down?"* Is it a quality or performance issue? Is it that you're getting pushed out by your competition? Do you really understand what your customers' needs are?

I've seen this scenario play out a few times, and each time, if the companies would've fixed what was ailing them, then sales numbers wouldn't be down. Don't take your eyes off the ball. Stay focused on the customer and the customer experience. Stay focused on the work that you're doing to improve the experience. After all, a poor experience is likely why customers aren't buying.

Problem #3: Misplaced Purpose

I've already written earlier in this chapter about the purpose of a business. But as you know, not every business owner or CEO aligns with Drucker's definition. Many still align with maximizing shareholder value, or worse yet, pure greed.

Sadly, the pharmaceutical industry has been accused of this latter practice many times in the last few years. Here's an example.

Check out this quote: *"I think it is a moral requirement to make money when you can . . . to sell the product for the highest price."*

That's an actual quote from an actual CEO. As a matter of fact, it's a quote from Nirmal Mulye, CEO of Nostrum Laboratories. He's defending his decision to raise the price of a drug five-fold to $2,400!

Nostrum Laboratories makes the generic version of a urinary tract infection (UTI) antibiotic (nitrofurantoin), which had sold for $474.75 until the price of the brand-name version (by Casper Pharma) of the drug rose to $2,800.

Mulye's response: *"The brand hiked the price. We are just trying to bring a cheaper alternative to the brand. So I'm the savior, not the villain, and everyone is making me the villain."*

"This is a capitalist economy and if you can't make money, you can't stay in business." He added: *"We have to make money when we can."*

He said that he is *"in this business to make money."* Clearly.

But what about the customer? And the impact on the customer?

Problem #4: Forgetting the Customer (is Human)

Remember the poor doctor being dragged off the United Airlines flight back in 2017? How can you forget? The images of the incident were cruel and gruesome.

There are plenty of other examples, but a great resource for other examples is Jeanne Bliss' book *Would You Do That to Your Mother?*

If there's ever a reason for me to write this book, Jeanne's book is it! In it, she outlines endless examples of how companies fail to put the customer in customer experience. Worse yet, in many cases, like the United Airlines example, they fail to treat people like humans! It's disgraceful. Did United Airlines actually consider the customer when it designed its policies?

As I go around the world speaking at events about these types of occurrences, I always pose this question: What happens to us as employees when we cross the threshold of our employers' offices? Where does our own humanity go? Does it get sucked out of us by the toxic air and toxic culture in which we work?

I'm afraid the answer to that last question is *"Yes."* But that's also for another book.

Speaking of treating customers like humans, when you have a spare sixty seconds, take a look at a commercial done by Acura a couple of years ago. The name of the commercial is "The Test," and it shows an Acura engineer testing the safety of the Acura MDX. As he places each crash-test dummy into the car, buckling them in and adjusting their seats, he imagines them as his own family: his wife, his daughter, and his son, and then it's revealed that he's envisioned himself as the driver. It's hauntingly realistic, and it will give you goosebumps. The tagline is: *"When you don't think of them as dummies, something amazing happens."*

Enough said.

Customers buy for their reasons, not yours. –Orwell Ray Wilson

ENDNOTES
Bain Delivery Gap: https://www.bain.com/insights/closing-the-delivery-gap-newsletter/

Wikipedia (Goodhart's Law):
https://en.wikipedia.org/wiki/Goodhart%27s_law

Nirmal Mulye's response:
https://www.kansascity.com/news/business/health-care/article218330465.html

Acura - The Test
https://www.youtube.com/watch?v=SkpaSe_Zj6o&feature=youtu.be

4 SHIFT HAPPENS

Customers can't and won't take it anymore! It's time to shift the focus. It's time to put the "customer" in *customer* experience.

But you can't just say *"We're going to 'do CX'"* and then "do CX." There's more to it than that!

Transforming the customer experience is much more complex than that simplified command. Transforming the customer experience requires a culture shift, a mindset shift, a behavioral shift. And that shift needs to come from—or start from—the top, from the executive staff, from your CEO.

Shift happens, right?

Yea, not so fast! Shift can't be forced. And it just doesn't happen on its own.

How does shift happen? What does that require? Unfortunately, as most customer experience professionals know, it requires some heavy lifting. In order to shift mindsets and behaviors, whether it's that of executives or of employees, you'll need to do the following . . .

- Be clear on what you are changing to; in other words, what is the current state? And what is the desired future state?

And why?

- Know and understand your audience: how do they learn? what motivates them?
- Frame the proposed shift in a way that they'll understand.
- Create context and tell a story: stories are a Trojan horse for learning.
- Build your business case.
- Start small and show some quick wins to help build momentum, to help get people on board (it won't happen all at once).
- Communicate clearly, openly, candidly, and regularly.
- Make sure that everyone knows the purpose, the vision, the goals, the desired outcomes—and that they understand the Why behind all of it—create a "greater cause" mentality.
- Regularly reinforce and reaffirm the change.

You've got to shift the thinking, as well as the messaging and the education, to "customer" and away from "us" or "we." That's critical.

Businesses can adopt one of two ways of thinking: inside out or outside in.

Inside-out thinking means your focus is on processes, systems, tools, and products that are designed and implemented based on internal thinking and intuition. The customer's needs, jobs, and perspectives do not play a part in this type of thinking; they aren't taken into consideration. You make decisions because you think it's what's best for the business—not for customers. Or you think you know what's best for customers.

On the other hand, **outside-in thinking** means that you look at your business from the customer's perspective and subsequently design processes, tools, and products and make decisions based on what's best for the customer and what meets the customer's needs. You make decisions because you know it's what's best for your customers. Why? Because you listen to them, and you understand them and the jobs they are trying to do.

It might be **inside-out thinking** when there's a conscious decision to make processes, policies, people, systems, or other changes that:

- Don't improve the customer experience at the same time
- Are about maximizing shareholder returns, not about benefits for the customer
- Improve internal efficiencies but to the detriment of customer interactions
- Are cost-cutting measures that also negatively impact the customer experience
- Might be the wrong process, policy, people, or systems to change

By contrast, **outside-in thinking** flips each of those points on its head and looks like this. There's a conscious decision to make processes, policies, people, systems, or other changes that:

- Improve the customer experience at the same time
- Are about maximizing benefits for the customer
- Improve internal efficiencies known to be pain points when executing customer interactions
- Are cost-cutting measures that significantly improve the customer experience
- Are the right process, policy, people, or systems because you've listened to customer feedback and know how customers are affected

It's clear that outside-in thinking is the way to go. It leads to a number of things, none of which you'll get by making decisions that are not based on what's best for your customers:

- Reduced complaints
- Increased satisfaction
- Increased referrals
- Increased repeat purchases
- Improved ease of doing business
- Fewer lost customers

These then translate to reduced costs and increased revenue for the business.

I wanted to spend a bit of time on this concept because outside-in thinking is at the core of putting the "customer" in *customer* experience.

***

Communication is, obviously, a huge part of making this shift a reality. Leaders must clearly communicate about the change:

- Why it's important to the audience and, ultimately, to the business
- That it's not a quick fix or the flavor of the day—it's a way of doing business from here on in
- How it affects each individual personally
- Give examples, including ROI
- How priorities have been redefined and why
- How it will be measured—and why
- Who's already on board; there's power in numbers, and it grows from there

You can expect pushback, but you have to just push through. This is important. Persistence is key. And yet, it's not enough. To drive lasting change, you've not only got to communicate the change vision and address each of those points, you've also got to:

- **Involve employees** in the change process rather than forcing change on them. If they're involved, the solutions may be richer because they have other ideas, perspectives, and experiences that the decision-making leader may not have. Better yet, present them with a problem or a situation, and let them come to the conclusion themselves. If they believe it was their own idea, it'll stick; they'll own it.
- Ensure that **executives lead by example and model the change** they wish to see from their employees; if they don't live the change, why should employees?! If your CEO doesn't demonstrate commitment to the transformation by being the role model for how to deliver a great experience, it

won't happen. If she doesn't live the core values, why should you? Actions always speak louder than words.

- **Recognize the right behaviors and reinforce** with incentives, promotions, success metrics, and more. Reinforcing the behaviors, actions, and changes that you want to see is more powerful than talking about them, especially when combined with modeling them.

Yes, change is hard. But it's not impossible.

***

That's a good segue into why mindset shifts, behavioral shifts, and culture shifts won't happen. I recently came across an article from Matthew E. May titled "20 Reasons Why Your Company Won't Change." Among the reasons Matt mentions, I've picked some of the most popular ones that I've seen or heard from other customer experience professionals and have listed them below. This explains a lot, but don't let it stop you! Push through it.

- **Fear**. We have an innate fear of the unknown. *"I'm afraid of what will happen."*
- **Myopia**. We can't see that change is in our broader self-interest. *"This won't help us."*
- **Selfishness**. Unless change immediately pays off for us, we'll resist it. *"What's in it for me?"*
- **Ego**. Those with power have to admit they've been wrong. *"I feel I've positioned us well for the future."*
- **Sleepwalking**. Too many people live unexamined lives. *"I just don't get it."*
- **Human nature**. We are naturally self-centered, and change requires some selflessness. *"Others will benefit more than me."*
- **Complacency**. We like the path of least resistance; we're not natural maximizers or optimizers. *"I'm satisfied with the way things are." "We've always done it this way."*
- **No constituency**. The power base of the status quo is greater than that of those trying to bring about change. *"There's no critical mass behind us."*

- **Short selling**. Perceived lack of knowledge, skills, tools, and experience. *"We've never done this; we don't know how to do this."*
- **Exceptionalism**. People can't see the situation objectively. *"That may work elsewhere, but we're different."*

What are you going to do? How are you going to "do CX?" How will you shift the culture, the mindset, and behaviors to make the customer the primary focus (after employees, of course) of your organization. What's stopping your company from making the shift? I'm sure you can come up with other reasons besides the ones listed on the previous page or others in Matt's article.

Faced with the choice between changing one's mind and proving that there is no need to do so, almost everyone gets busy on the proof. –John Kenneth Galbraith, Professor of Economics, Harvard University

ENDNOTES
Source for Matthew E. May's article:
http://www.innovationexcellence.com/blog/2017/07/09/20-reasons-why-your-company-wont-change/

5 FOUNDATION OF CX TRANSFORMATION SUCCESS

Make no mistake about it: customers expect you to transform your business to one that is customer-focused and customer-centric. (Maybe not in so many words, but their expectations are high.) But clearly, you can't do that without knowing what the foundational elements of customer experience transformation success are.

When they are missing in your organization, I refer to them as the "Deadly Sins of Customer Experience." Deadly sins are mortal sins—they are the origins or roots of other vices; so do these things wrong, and you'll only end up with a domino effect.

Executive Conviction and Commitment
If executives aren't on board with focusing on the customer, then forget it; it won't happen. You might have localized or departmentalized efforts, but those will be siloed efforts that translate to siloed experiences for the customer. Without executive commitment, you'll never get resources—human, capital, financial, or other—to execute on your customer experience strategy.

And it's important to know that there is a difference between buy-in and commitment. You want commitment! You don't want lip service. A client recently made me chuckle when she told me that her CEO is wearing the (metaphorical) t-shirt but doesn't know what CX means or what it stands for. (That's buy-in.)

So what's the difference between buy-in and commitment? Let me tell you a quick story to help you relate. Have you heard the one about the pig and the chicken?

> *A Pig and a Chicken are walking down the road.*
> *Chicken says: "Hey, Pig. I was thinking we should open a restaurant!"*
> *Pig replies: "Hmm, maybe. What would we call it?"*
> *Chicken responds: "How about Ham-n-Eggs?"*
> *Pig thinks for a moment and says: "No, thanks. I'd be committed, but you'd only be involved."*

Think about that for a second.

As Ken Blanchard says: *"There's a difference between interest and commitment. When you're interested in something, you do it only when it's convenient. When you're committed to something, you accept no excuses—only results."*

Commitment, obviously, means that you're all in. It's the act of committing or promising to do something, e.g., committing resources, as mentioned earlier.

Conviction, on the other hand, is a firmly-held belief. You believe in the customer experience. You believe the customer is at the center or at the core of your business. You believe the customer is and must be recognized as the reason you are in business. Conviction is a strong word. We need more CEOs with a customer-centric conviction.

Whether you've got commitment or conviction—or both—you know and understand what is required to undertake this transformation, and you deliberately designed a customer-centric culture that begins with ensuring you've got the right values in place. Customer experience transformation really begins with a culture transformation. Without a customer-centric culture, without a culture that lives and breathes putting the customer into everything the business does, it's going to be hard to transform the customer experience. That culture, that thinking—it starts from the top.

That's a good segue into the next foundational element.

Culture

Culture is defined as Values + Behavior. Core values are the fundamental beliefs of the organization; they really describe or define the culture. Core values are broad statements that guide your employees, identifying right and wrong, good and bad, and how to interact with each other and with customers.

As Roy Disney said, *"It's not hard to make decisions when you know what your values are."* Those decisions include who to hire, fire, and promote. To facilitate that decision-making process, core values must also be enriched with examples of desired behaviors that align with each core value and then linked to desired outcomes. This is an exercise often forgotten by organizations (or they don't even realize they need to do this), which results in core values falling flat and being ignored.

Mission, Vision, Purpose

You must have all of your core business statements, as I like to call them, defined and communicated. The mission statement describes the business you are in, i.e., what you're doing and who you're serving, while the vision statement defines where the company wants to go in the future. By the way, the corporate vision and the customer experience vision ought to be aligned—or even the same.

The company's purpose is its reason for being, the why. It's typically stated in such a way that helps employees understand who the business is trying to impact and in what way. Employees are inspired when they know they are doing something for the good of something or someone else.

Brand Promise

Your brand promise is the expectation you set with your customers; in essence, it's a promise you make to your customers about the experience and the benefit they can expect from engaging with your brand. Everything you and your employees do should reflect this promise. It's a combination of the brand purpose and the reality of what the brand can deliver. It defines the benefits a customer can expect to receive when experiencing your brand at every touchpoint.

Leadership Alignment

In addition to executive commitment, all executives and all leaders (not just executive staff) must be aligned on the journey—and the goals of the journey—that lies ahead. If they aren't, it will likely be a challenge to ensure this is an enterprise-wide effort, which it must be. The good news is that there are ways to bring them all along and get them in a place where they will work together for the greater good. (That's another book.)

Just know this: commitment and alignment are different. I just explained commitment earlier in this chapter. Alignment means that everyone is on the same page. Alignment means that they have chosen to commit and support each other in the goal. They may not always agree, but at the end of the day, they walk the walk and talk the talk. They don't bad-mouth the transformation; they support it—and advocate for it—through thick and thin.

CX Governance

Without governance in place as a building block of your customer experience transformation, you perpetuate silo thinking and fail to achieve cross-functional alignment, adoption, involvement, and commitment.

CX governance has two components: the governance structure and the operating model. The *governance structure* outlines people, roles, and responsibilities when it comes to your customer experience strategy. The *operating model* has clearly-defined rules and guidelines for how the customer experience management strategy will be executed.

Governance is about a governing body, policies, monitoring, accountability, and enhancing the prosperity of the organization. In a nutshell, governance is about both oversight and execution. This is an important foundation for your customer experience management strategy. You really can't make this stuff up as you go along; there needs to be a formal structure in place.

In terms of oversight, the governance structure outlines people, roles, and responsibilities. Which teams and committees are going to ensure that there is alignment and accountability across the organization? We often see this piece of the governance structure refer to a core program team, an executive sponsor, an executive committee, cross-functional champions, and a culture committee. Your governance structure should include the teams of people you believe will best champion the strategy, driven by your corporate and customer experience vision, for your organization.

The governance committees will be important to getting organization adoption and alignment around the vision, strategy, and the work to be done. They will be critical to achieving that grassroots groundswell of customer-centricity. And they will help break down or connect silos.

With regards to the operating model portion of governance, there must be clearly-defined rules and guidelines for how the customer experience management strategy will be executed. Who will drive the efforts and how? How will you transform to a customer-centric culture? How will organizational adoption be achieved? How do you train, coach, and continue to motivate employees to focus on the customer? How will you listen to customers? Who will use the data and how? Where does accountability lie? What processes and policies must be in place in order to roll out these efforts? What is your decision-making process? How will you prioritize improvement opportunities? How will change management be handled? How will you measure success? How does it all link or connect to your desired business outcomes?

Organization Adoption, and Alignment

Obviously, this transformation work isn't going to get done by itself. It does take a village. (Ugh, sorry.) Employees must be on board with the transformation. They've got to understand what it is, why it's happening, and what it means for them.

There are several different ways to get that adoption and alignment, including:

- Communicate the vision but also communicate the who, what, when, where, why, and how. Don't hide anything or mask it as something it's not. Be open and honest.
- Teach them about customers and the experience today. The customer understanding concepts that I'll be addressing in this book are critical to providing clarity and understanding for employees.
- Provide a clear line of sight to the customer. When employees know how their contributions matter, when they know how what they do impacts the customer experience, that makes all the difference in the world.
- Involve employees in the whole process (from understanding through design, implementation, and delivery) rather than forcing or imposing the work on them.
- Empower them to deliver the experience customers expect.
- Make sure they know that their experience, the employee experience, is important and that their needs will be addressed at the same time.

One of the important concepts that they need to grasp is that this isn't about more work for them—this isn't another project on their plates. This is about a new way of working, a more efficient way, a better way; it's better because you're doing things for the customer because of the customer, which in the end is better for the business too.

Customer Understanding

You can't transform something you don't understand. Included in that "understanding" is not only the current state of the experience but also (especially) the customer himself. I won't go into this in any detail here because this is what the rest of the book is about.

Employee Experience

I define employee experience as the sum of all interactions that an employee has with her employer during the duration of her employment "relationship"—plus the actions and capabilities (tools resources, processes, training, workspace, workplace) that enable her to do her job, and especially, the feelings, emotions, and perceptions the employee has about those interactions and capabilities.

Quite simply, without employees, you have no customer experience; the employee experience drives the customer experience.

While you'll read a lot about putting the customer first, employees must be "more first." (Thanks to Hal Rosenbluth for that way of looking at this hierarchy.) Leaders must care for their employees, i.e., truly care about them as people, as humans. They must coach, develop, recognize, and appreciate them. And they must ensure that they have the right tools, resources, processes, policies, and training to do their jobs well and to serve their customers the way that customers deserve and desire to be served. Why? Because that's what employees have told me they need!

I could write an entire book on this topic alone (Okay, how many other books have I committed to writing so far?!), but I'll leave it at that for now. And as I mentioned earlier, all of the customer understanding concepts that I discuss in this book apply to the employee experience too.

***

The last concepts that I'm writing about are CX vision and strategy. They are not foundational elements; they are outputs of all of the foundational elements I just wrote about. Once you've got those elements in place, you'll see why I need to mention these two here.

CX Vision and Strategy

You must have a customer experience vision and strategy. Your customer experience vision, which is grounded in customer feedback and insights, will be inspirational and aspirational and will outline what you see as the future state of the customer experience. It will briefly describe the experience you plan to deliver. And it will serve as a guide to help choose future courses of action. That little statement packs a lot of punch! The customer experience strategy outlines your approach to delivering a great experience, to delivering on that vision.

Having a vision shows you understand it's a journey. Developing a strategy lets your employees know how you're going to get there. Some customer experience vision tips include:

- The vision will guide your strategy.
- Strategy drives execution and subsequent actions.
- Business decisions should be made based on this vision.
- It is internal.
- It must be communicated.
- It must have commitment and buy-in from those who live it, execute on it (shared vision).
- All employees must know how they contribute to, and align with, the vision.
- The vision should motivate, inspire.
- Revisit it at a regular interval to ensure that it still reflects the experience you want to deliver.

An important side note: Your company vision is an inspirational and aspirational statement that outlines what the company is trying to achieve near term and long term; it also guides decision-making processes and subsequent, resultant courses of action. Your vision will (a) draw the line between what you're doing and for whom you're doing it and (b) create alignment within the organization. **Your customer experience vision and your company vision are always linked, and often one and the same**. Without this north star, employees can easily go off track and focus on projects or ideas that aren't critical to what the business is trying to do.

Companies that change may survive, but companies that transform thrive. Change brings incremental or small-scale adaptations, while transformation brings great improvements that ripple through the future of an organization. –Nick Candito

6 CUSTOMER UNDERSTANDING

You can't transform something you don't understand. (Yes! I will repeat this throughout the book!) If you don't know and understand what the current state of the customer experience is—especially what's going well and what isn't—how can you possibly design the desired future state?

Customer understanding is the cornerstone of customer-centricity.

A lot of executives talk about being customer-centric, but it's one thing to say that and another to be it! Customer-centricity is about putting the customer at the center of all you do.

Customer-centric companies ensure that they make no decisions, design no products and services, and implement no processes without first thinking of the customer and the impact that the decision or the design has on the customer. They ask, *"How will this impact the customer? How will it make her feel? Does it add value, or does it create pain?"*

In customer-centric companies, decisions are always made with the customer's best interests in mind. The customer's voice is brought into meetings and into conversations; the customer is always represented. Jeff Bezos' empty chair concept is a great example of this and has been widely adopted by other brands.

It's important to note that a customer experience transformation can only happen when there is a commitment (and conviction) to change the culture to one that is customer-centric, even customer-obsessed.

Being customer-centric happens by design. Customer-centric companies do the following to ensure the organization knows its reason for being, i.e., the customer, and to embed the customer into the DNA of the organization. They . . .

- Have visible (and visibly) customer-centric leadership, demonstrating a customer commitment from the top down
- Develop and socialize customer personas
- Speak and think in the customer's language
- Use customer feedback and data to better understand their customers
- Are engaged in continuous improvement as a result of the customer understanding efforts
- Focus on products and services that deliver value for their customers, i.e., solving their problems and helping them with jobs to be done
- Have a commitment to customer success
- Engage with customers from the beginning
- Walk in the customer's shoes to understand today's experience in order to design a better experience for tomorrow
- Foster a customer-centric culture
- Empower the frontline to do what's right for the customer
- Ensure all employees (front line and back office) understand how they impact the customer and her experience
- Recognize the customer across all channels
- Design processes and policies from the customer's point of view
- Measure what matters to customers
- Encourage customer innovation
- Include customer-driven values in their core values
- Recruit and hire employees passionate about customers and

about helping customers

- Incorporate the customer and the customer experience into their onboarding processes
- Train employees on how to deliver the experience that customers expect
- Establish a customer room that is open to employees 24/7 so that they can learn more about their customers and the customer experience
- Rewards and recognition reinforce employee behaviors that align with customer-centricity
- Have a C-suite executive who champions the customer across the entire organization
- Customers before metrics, i.e., every meeting begins with and includes customer stories
- Invest in the latest technology to support and deliver the experience customers expect

As you can see, becoming a customer-centric organization is a commitment that requires a mindset shift and a behavior shift, which I wrote about in the previous chapter, and especially, some investments—financial, human, time, resources, technology, and more.

Becoming a customer-centric organization means that you're going to deliberately put the "customer" in *customer* experience and, especially, into the business.

Putting the customer into customer experience means that you are going to consider the customer and the impact on the customer for every decision you make: business decisions, product decisions, service decisions, support decisions, digital decisions, and more!

That translates to: all decisions must be grounded in data, insights, and customer understanding, meaning you're going to understand customers' needs, pain points, jobs to be done, and problems to solve, and then co-create better experiences with them; in return, you'll achieve the desired business outcomes.

That's how you put the customer in customer experience—and

at the center of all you do: via customer understanding.

There are three main ways to achieve understanding—and each one includes a wealth of data. (Hold that thought.)

1. **Listen**. Don't just ask customers about the experience, listen as well. There are a lot of different channels and ways for customers to tell you about their needs and desired outcomes and how well you are performing against their expectations. Understanding these expectations and identifying key drivers of a great customer experience are important outcomes of this exercise. Note that listening also includes the breadcrumbs of data that customers leave as they touch and interact with your brand.

2. **Characterize**. Research customers. Identify who they are, what jobs they are trying to do, and what problems they are trying to solve. Compile key personas that represent various types of prospects and customers that (might) buy from you or use your products and services.

3. **Empathize**. Walk in your customers' shoes to understand the steps they take to do whatever it is they are trying to do with your organization. Map their journeys to understand the current state of the experience from the customer's viewpoint.

All three of these approaches are closely linked. Both Listen (feedback) and Characterize (personas) result in a lot of data that feed into the maps (Empathize). Here's some proof.

MyCustomer.com conducted research in 2018 in which they uncovered two interesting stats:

- 60% of companies that don't journey map are not satisfied with the insights they have into customer journeys.
  - They are only surveying or using other listening posts.
- 89% of companies that use journey maps are satisfied or very satisfied with the insights.
  - They conduct customer research, incorporate voice of the customer feedback, and enrich their maps with customer data.

All three of these concepts are learning exercises, critical learning exercises. You walk away from each one of them with a lot of knowledge about customers and about the experience they desire. When combined, you are so much wiser and have a greater understanding of customers and of the work that lies ahead. And that is key: you've got to do something with what you learn. This action is where customer understanding manifests itself into customer-centricity and becomes the cornerstone for it.

To be successful, you'll need to make sure you truly understand what you've heard from and about customers, their needs, and their expectations. Without that understanding, the exercises have failed. Make sure they're done right.

I'll help you do that as I go into much more detail about all three in the following chapters. A couple tips, though, to kick it off:

- When you listen, ask the right questions at the right time of the right audience to elicit the feedback you need to understand what's going right and what isn't. And then do something with it.
- When you characterize, first and foremost, do the research, and then ensure that the research is rooted in the right data, i.e., relevant prospect and customer data and interviews.
- And when you empathize, when you walk in your customer's shoes to understand his experience, you need to make sure you capture the experience from his viewpoint because creating it from yours defeats the purpose of this process. And then, you've got fix what's wrong.

The rest of the book will cover these three concepts, with the largest chunk being devoted to the third, Empathize (journey mapping).

Understanding human needs is half the job of meeting them. – Adlai E. Jr. Stevenson

LISTEN

7 LISTEN TO CUSTOMERS

When it comes to customer understanding, listening is where most companies start. As you know, companies survey customers for every interaction and transaction under the sun. I would not recommend this "every interaction and transaction" approach for your customer listening strategy, but it's important that you bring the voice of the customer into the organization.

Net-net: listening is a good place to start. Do it in a way that is coordinated and not frustrating for your customers. Remember, the survey is another touchpoint of the customer experience.

There are typically two approaches that companies take when launching voice of the customer programs; they either ask or listen.

- **Ask**. This is all about reaching out to customers to ask questions about things you want to know about them and their experience. Example methods of asking include: transactional or relationship surveys, market and marketing research surveys, focus groups, online communities, 1:1 interviews, and customer advisory boards.

- **Listen**. Don't just ask customers about the experience, listen as well. Let customers tell you about their needs and desired outcomes and how well you are performing against their expectations in whatever method or channel they want to. Example listening approaches include: online reviews, social media, ethnographic research and immersion programs, customer advisory boards (yes, they belong in both buckets, ask and listen), and voice of the customer through the employee. Another way you can listen is via the breadcrumbs of data that customers leave everywhere they touch your business, e.g., website, customer service calls, purchase transactions, etc. In other words, operational, behavioral, and transactional data are another way to "listen" to customers.

***

Where to begin? If you're new to this whole customer understanding and customer experience thing and haven't got any formal processes and programs in place—but know you need to start—it's important to understand what your goals are for doing so. Don't listen just for the sake of listening; too many companies do that.

When you establish a voice of the customer program, you must begin with the same things with which you start any other initiative or program: objectives, desired outcomes for the customer and for the business, and success metrics. (And executive commitment. But from here on out, I'm going to assume you have that.) Design with the end in mind. If you don't know where you're going, how will you know when you get there? And if you can't measure that you've arrived, you'll just never know if you did, will you?

Some of the typical, high-level desired outcomes include:

For the business
- Increased revenue
- Reduced costs
- Reduced sales cycle (faster)
- Culture change

For the customer
- Reduced effort
- Increased satisfaction
- Expectations met
- Improved experience
- Value achieved

More on outcomes and how to measure them in Chapter 12.

***

If you're *not* new to this customer understanding and customer experience thing, you will likely benefit from stepping back for a moment and creating a feedback map.

Every department in your company thirsts for feedback from customers to help measure brand awareness, design products, improve service offerings, understand satisfaction levels, and more. Unfortunately, more often than not, there is no coordinated effort across the organization to ensure that: (a) customers are not over-surveyed, which can be defined either as being surveyed too frequently, i.e., no-touch rules, or asked the same or similar questions by different departments; (b) you respond to feedback wherever customers provide it, e.g., online reviews, etc.; or (c) the feedback is collected, analyzed, and used in a cohesive fashion.

Think about the many customer touchpoints with your organization, and then think about the various departments in your organization that might be asking customers for feedback at each of those touchpoints. It can be quite overwhelming—for you and for your customers! To make sense of it all, you should compile a customer feedback map to align with your customer journey map.

Creating a customer feedback map can be a daunting task, especially in very large, disparate, and/or siloed organizations, but the benefits—not the least of which is financial—are endless. For example, if you have nine different departments all working in a vacuum, including licensing nine different survey, enterprise feedback management, or text analytics platforms, consolidating the data can reduce costs and improve the way the company listens to customers. Other benefits include reducing or eliminating respondent fatigue, increasing response rates, and improving the actionability of the data.

The customer feedback map should first identify your touchpoints and the corresponding departments that support each. Start with a customer lifecycle map that highlights the lifecycle stages and then inventories the many and various touchpoints within each stage. In other words, create a touchpoint map. You can do this in Google Sheets—or you can start with butcher paper and sticky notes—in order to bring multiple people together to contribute to this exercise.

On the map, mark each touchpoint at or for which you're gathering feedback. You might even color code the touchpoint red, yellow, or green, depending on satisfaction scores.

Next, you'll add details to the map, including:

- All forms/sources of customer feedback at each touchpoint
- Other feedback the may be indirectly linked to a touchpoint
- Owner of the feedback
- Audience for each piece of feedback
- End-user (internal) of the feedback
- Objective/purpose of the feedback
- All resources used for feedback/analysis (software, tools, etc.)
- Desired sources of feedback (gaps)

This can then also be the first step toward mapping the interaction and transaction data that you capture (in your contact center, CRM, or other similar platform) about customers at each of those touchpoints as well, creating a comprehensive picture of all of the data you have on your customers.

After you've created the feedback map, the next step is to consolidate your listening efforts. Centralizing to one department both the ownership of your voice of the customer efforts and the platform used to collect, analyze, and respond to the feedback eliminates redundancies, creates efficiencies, saves money, and ensures a cohesive approach to your voice of the customer program overall and, ultimately, to the customer experience.

Identifying the various sources of customer feedback within your organization is a valuable exercise. You may just discover some very scary information: how much your customers are being asked to provide feedback—and just how little of that is actually being used in a meaningful way.

The hardest thing is being able to put your ego aside so that you can learn. We all want to create what's in our head, but you need to be able to put your own ideas to the side and really listen to your customers to solve their problems. –David Cancel

8 ACTIONABLE DATA

Whoever said, *"Data that is not actionable is just data"* was spot on. Let's start there. In order to take action, your data must first be actionable: you have to be able to act on it.

So you've been running your voice of the customer program for the last couple of years, and you're frustrated because you can't seem to move the needle on the customer experience. Questions like these run through your head: Why are our customers still unhappy? Why is the service our company delivers so bad? When will those product issues be resolved? Why don't our customers recommend our company? Why don't they buy again? What's going on?

You need to get to the root cause of this situation.

I think I can safely narrow it down to this: your surveys. Don't be offended. I've seen a lot of bad surveys over the last twenty-five years, and I can tell you that if you don't get them right, it'll be a challenge to improve anything.

Consider this: Are you asking the right questions? Are the (right) questions you're asking actionable? Do you know what to do with the feedback you're getting?

In order to improve the customer experience, you definitely

need to listen to your customers. That's a given. You need to understand who they are and what they are trying to do. And how well you're helping them achieve what they're trying to do. But you need to be sure to structure your survey questions in such a way that the feedback is meaningful and actionable, that it truly helps you understand the experience and how well you're helping the customer do what he needs to do.

When you're designing your surveys, are you thinking "actionable?" Are you employing "actionability thinking?"

What does that mean?

When you're thinking "actionable," you're considering the following as you propose and design the questions:

- What will we do if this question is rated low (or high)?
- How will we act on it?
- Who owns this question?
- Who else needs this information?
- Who will act on it?
- How quickly can we make changes?
- Is this something we can actually change?
- Why are we asking this?

Asking for feedback about something you can't change—or in such a way that you're not sure what you need to change—is pointless. You're wasting both your customers' time and your company's time. If you can't succinctly answer these "actionability" questions, then reconsider what you're asking.

Once you've thought about—and clearly answered—these higher-level questions, it's time to think about question design. How are you going to ask your survey questions to ensure that you can effect real change in the customer experience?

Here are a few survey design tips using the "actionable thinking" approach to make sure you're asking meaningful questions.

1. Don't ask double-barreled or compound questions.

If you're not familiar with this phrase, I'll give you an example: *"How satisfied are you with the speed and quality of the solution you were given?"* You're asking about speed of the solution and quality of the solution, two very distinct things. First, this will confuse the respondent. What if speed was great but the quality wasn't? Or vice versa? Next, it will frustrate whoever needs to act on it because it's not clear what needs to be fixed, one or the other or both. Keep your questions to just one thought/concept.

2. Don't ask leading or biased questions.

"We know you loved our new soft drink. How much did you love it?" Okay, silly example, but you get the point. Don't bias the question wording by putting a positive or negative spin on it. Simply ask what you want to ask; don't lead the witness.

3. Don't ask generic, high-level questions that aren't specific enough to drive change.

Asking customers to *"rate your overall satisfaction with our website"* without additional, detailed attributes about the site or without an open-ended question to understand the why behind the rating is not helpful.

4. For open-ended questions, be specific.

Ask exactly what you want to know, e.g., *"What can we do to ensure you rate us a 10 on overall satisfaction the next time you do business with us?"* or, *"Tell us the single most important reason you recommended us to your friends."* Be sure to ask one question that is a little more open so that customers can share feedback about what they want you to know versus what you want to know, e.g., *"Please use this space to provide any additional feedback you'd like to share with us."*

5. Make sure your questions are not ambiguous.

Write questions clearly. If a respondent pauses and says, *"What do they mean by that?"* then the question is poorly constructed. Poorly-constructed questions result in responses that are not actionable; nobody really knows what they mean.

6. Your question response choices and rating scales should be mutually exclusive.

When response choices overlap or don't make sense, they become meaningless, and that means they are also not actionable.

7. Do your homework.

Make sure you provide a complete list of response choices. I hate when the one answer that should be there is missing. Be sure to provide an "Other (please specify)" when appropriate. Not offering this latter option either forces people to skip the question or to select something that may not be accurate—and that's not actionable; it's misleading.

8. Only ask questions that are relevant to that customer and his experience.

Don't mix in a bunch of marketing research questions or other nice-to-knows. Those questions are out of context and are also not relevant to what you're trying to achieve, which means they aren't actionable for your cause.

9. For future question ideas, review verbatims for emerging and actionable topics.

These verbatims are a rich source of information, for a variety of reasons!

If you really want to improve the customer experience, then you need to start with good data! You need to ask the right questions: relevant, meaningful, and actionable questions. Then analyze to identify the key drivers and next best actions. And don't forget to act!

Genius is in the idea. Impact, however, comes from action. – Simon Sinek

9 ANALYZE FOR ACTION

While listening is about hearing how your customers feel about your products and services and the experience you deliver, the most important part of listening is to hear what was said, and then do something with what you heard.

Asking and listening both yield a ton of data, in both structured and unstructured formats. And when combined with what you capture about customers during their transactions and interactions with your brand, you've got a wealth of knowledge about your customers. Now you need to do something with that.

Customers expect easy, effortless, seamless, convenient, relevant, consistent, and personalized experiences. You hold in your hands the keys to making that happen.

Once you've inventoried your feedback and data (see Chapter 7), it's time to transform it into a usable format so that the business can consume it and affect the customer experience in a positive way. My six steps for transforming and consuming the data are as follows.

1. Data must first be **centralized**. Data is useless to improving the customer experience when it remains siloed; siloed data means siloed experiences. You cannot deliver a personalized customer experience across your various channels if the data is housed in several disparate systems. You need a way to bring the data

together in one place so that it can be analyzed in a sane way. Data warehouses and data lakes are above my pay grade, but I know that this is where the data must reside for easy, centralized access.

2. Data must be **analyzed**. Analysis takes many forms because there will be many different types of data to make sense of. You'll need a way to crosstab, predict, identify key drivers, and prioritize improvements with survey data; mine and analyze your unstructured data; and track, review, and prioritize social media inputs and influencers. You'll conduct linkage analysis to link customer and employee data, customer feedback with operational metrics, and all data to financial measures. And you'll need to conduct a root cause analysis to understand the why behind it all.

3. Data must be **synthesized**. Once data has been broken down and analyzed for better understanding, it is most useful for the end-user when transformed into insights. Put all of the pieces of the analysis together to tell a story; to put it into context for those who need to act on it—a story that can be easily understood and translated into a better customer experience.

4. Data must be **socialized**. Those insights and their corresponding stories must be shared across the organization in such a way that people know what to do with it. Insights and resultant recommendations must get into the hands of the right people who will do something with them.

5. Data must be **strategized**. To strategize means to define your strategy or your action plan, and in this case, it involves both tactical (how you'll respond to each and every customer) and strategic (how the business will respond, including operational, product, and process changes) measures. This is where you turn insights into action.

6. Data must be **operationalized**. Ensure that you have the right feedback at the right time from the right customers then glean insights, create action plans, and drive it all back to the right departments and right employees who take action, e.g., update or revamp policies and processes, train employees, upgrade tools and systems, change their delivery approach, deliver relevant

messaging, etc. at the right touchpoints at the right time. Then close the loop on your own change management process: track and measure your efforts in order to maintain a continuous improvement cycle.

I might make this sound simple and simplistic. I know it's not. Challenges arise from the get-go, especially as you try to identify the data sources and as you run up against silos and other issues. Using tools like customer journey maps, customer feedback maps, and a general data architecture/map can help to bring it all into focus. It's then important to conduct the proper analysis to uncover the issues to solve to achieve the desired outcomes. That's a good segue into analytics.

***

Data is available in abundance these days. There are a ton of statistics out there about the volume of data we see today versus just a few years ago, but I think we can all agree that there's a lot of it! And I think we can all agree that most companies don't use—or don't know how to use—even a tenth of it.

Of the six steps you just read about, most companies get hung up on the first step. And if they know where their data is and have pulled it all into a data lake, or if they've gotten as much data together as they believe they can for now, they then get stuck on the next step, analyze. This is where I think there is a real opportunity for customer experience professionals. This is where we've got some new tools.

Which tools?

Companies are sitting on a goldmine of data. It's time to do something with all of that data. It's time to forecast the future and remedy the present. What am I talking about? Predictive analytics and, more importantly, prescriptive analytics. These are two important tools that customer experience professionals must have in their toolboxes today and into the future. Unfortunately, many of these professionals are still either unaware of the tools or aren't sure what they (can) do.

Traditionally, companies were able to identify and prioritize improvement opportunities from their customer surveys via correlation or regression analysis and quadrant charts, which identify priority improvements, table stakes, and things to continue doing. But I don't think—actually, I know—a lot of folks put faith into those quadrant charts, which don't offer up the ability to identify the impact those improvements (or the "continue doings") would have on the desired business outcomes.

In recent years, there's been an evolution from purely descriptive analytics (basic, summary statistics) to predictive analytics (predicting some future outcome based on what you know about the customer or on historical data). And now, you have prescriptive analytics, which takes that prediction and tells you why and then what to do, outlining the next best action to take in order to achieve a desired outcome.

According to Wikipedia, prescriptive analytics:

"not only anticipates what will happen and when it will happen but also why it will happen. Further, prescriptive analytics suggests decision options on how to take advantage of a future opportunity or mitigate a future risk and shows the implication of each decision option. Prescriptive analytics can continually take in new data to re-predict and re-prescribe, thus automatically improving prediction accuracy and prescribing better decision options. Prescriptive analytics ingests hybrid data, a combination of structured (numbers, categories) and unstructured (videos, images, sounds, texts) data and business rules to predict what lies ahead and to prescribe how to take advantage of this predicted future without compromising other priorities."

You can already see how this is a windfall for customer experience professionals and, more importantly, for customers.

Prescriptive analytics isn't just for survey data, though. If you've got customer demographic, transaction, interaction, or other behavioral data, you can analyze it as well (or in combination with survey data) to predict not only some outcome but also which customers (down to the individual customer) will most likely be aligned with that outcome, and then use prescriptive analytics to prescribe the next course of action to take with each customer to ensure the outcome is achieved.

In plain English, here's an example: first, you predict who is most likely to buy a certain type of car, and then prescriptive analytics identifies which experience, messaging, discounts, offers, sales approach, etc. to use to take the customer over the line and make the purchase.

Customers want personalized experiences; this is one tool, one method, to use to ensure that happens. Use prescriptive analytics to take your customer data to the next level, improving the experience and adding value for your customers.

I've often said that data is just data until you do something with it. You need a tool to identify the what: what is it that you're supposed to do with the data? Ultimately, you need those prescriptive analytics to identify why, how, and where—from which action—you'll get the biggest bang for your buck.

Having prescriptive analytics in your customer experience toolbox gives you a huge, first-mover advantage. There's still a large awareness and education effort required to help companies realize the beauty and the benefits of using prescriptive analytics to transform the customer experience, especially the part about personalizing the experience down to the individual level.

If you've been stuck in a rut and haven't been able to make any progress toward improving the customer experience, it's time to rethink how you've been analyzing your data. Making data-driven decisions will only lead to better outcomes—for the customer and for the business. In July 2017, a survey by Workday and *The Economist* found that 59 percent of respondents who described their organization as "data-driven" said their company is more profitable than competitors, compared to 40 percent who said they do not work in a data-driven environment.

Let's get you into that "more profitable" bucket! Let's talk action.

Better yet. Let's act!

But. And it's a big but . . .

"Insights without action are just expensive trivia." –Unknown

ENDNOTES
Source for Wikipedia definition:
https://en.wikipedia.org/wiki/Prescriptive_analytics

10 SOCIALIZE THE INSIGHTS

I love this quote from Lolly Daskal: *"Insight alone does not cause change. Change requires action."* This couldn't be truer—in life and, especially, in customer experience transformations. And to that I add, *"Nothing changes if nothing changes."* So let's change some things!

There's a lot of research out there that supports the fact that companies just aren't using the data that they have available in-house to design and deliver a better experience for customers. You can analyze your data ad nauseam, but if you do nothing with it, you're no better off—and neither are your customers.

Customer listening programs are successful—drive desired outcomes—when you make improvements based on what you hear, close the loop, and let customers and employees in on it.

In order for data and insights to be acted upon, they must first be socialized; they must first get into the hands of the right people who can then make good use of them.

The first step toward action is to close the loop. There are five different ways to close the loop on your feedback, or on the insights, with customers and with employees.

1. Close the loop at the personal level.

Also known as service recovery, this is one of the most important ways to follow up with customers about their feedback; it lets them know that their opinions matter and that you are committed to improving the experience. The business benefits through customer retention, reduced negative word of mouth, product enhancements/ideas, and potential growth opportunities.

Outline a systematic approach for service recovery to occur at the individual customer level. Who will respond to the customer? Within what timeframe? In what mode (phone, email, in-person)? What will they say/ask (e.g., apologize, ask for more information to get to the root cause, schedule a follow-up call for more details, etc.)? How will you empower your staff to handle these calls? What information do they need in order to make the call? What is the intended outcome of the follow-up? When and how does the service recovery get escalated? How will you capture the discussion? Will you share best practices with others to learn from? How will you know if the customer is satisfied with the follow-up? How will you know if you've "saved" the customer?

2. Close the loop at the tactical level.

By tactical level, I'm referring to closing the loop with stakeholders, with those teams or departments with a vested interest in the specific feedback. Share the feedback with them so that they can address the following: What are some of the common issues, themes, or trends that arise from the data? How can/will each department respond to their respective issues? What will they fix? What improvements do they need to make to their specific policies and processes? What additional training does their staff require? What tools do they need? What communication is required to ensure the entire team or department is on board with the required changes? Are there best practices that they can share with other departments?

3. Close the loop at the strategic level.

Acting at the personal and tactical levels is paramount, but it's also necessary to step back and look at the big picture. Some of the improvements that need to be made are organization-wide and require C-level involvement to ensure the commitment is there for time, funds, and other resources. They'll need to view the insights you gain from customers under a larger lens: Are there common feedback themes across the organization? What structural changes does the entire business need to make? How should we incorporate the feedback into our decision-making processes? How can the feedback influence business performance and strategies? What communications are required to engage the organization in a more-strategic overhaul or transformation?

4. Close the loop with employees.

If employees don't know what they're doing wrong, then they can't change their own actions and behaviors. Your employees are the ones who deliver the customer experience; keeping them in the dark about how they are performing or how they are meeting customers' needs is detrimental to the business. They have the ability to immediately change the customer's experience, so share the feedback with them. Recognize them for the right behaviors and for delighting customers. Or coach them when the experience didn't go so well.

5. Close the loop with customers.

This is a must! Again, customers spend their precious time providing you feedback about your products and services; the least you can do is tell them what you did with their feedback, what improvements you made as a result, including both tactical and strategic changes. Communicating this to customers reassures them that: their feedback is valuable, their time wasn't wasted, you actually use their feedback, and they can provide feedback again. Always communicate back to your customers what changes were made as a result of their feedback and thank them for taking the time to do so. Given that this type of communication is more global in nature than personalized service recovery, it will cover more-strategic improvements but may also cover some of the tactical changes that you've made. Either way, don't forget this piece of communication.

One key point to keep in mind: remember that closing the loop is not just about acknowledging, addressing, and resolving the bad experiences. We tend to focus on the bad and how to make it better, but close the loop on the good too. Celebrate the good. If the feedback is positive, thank your customers and perhaps delve deeper into why they would promote your brand; activate your advocates, share the good news internally to highlight what a good experience looks like, and give kudos and recognition to employees where due.

Some companies close one of these loops but not the others; some companies do none of these. They are all critical. Do them all. Hardwiring customer feedback into your operational processes, whether tactical or strategic, and into meetings, discussions, and business decisions is the only way you'll get value and results out of your voice of the customer program. Using customer feedback for continuous improvement at the various levels outlined above ensures voice of the customer program success.

There are multiple other ways to socialize your insights (not just from listening but also from characterizing and empathizing), but be sure to tailor the delivery method and the insights to the audience and the expected and desired outcome.

1. Role-based or individual **dashboards** in your CRM system, VoC platform, or other data democratization platforms give the right people access to the right data and insights.
2. **CX Champions** can help to get the insights out into their respective departments; they'll know how to best communicate, socialize, and operationalize with their teams.
3. Get on the agenda of your **executive team staff meeting** and brief them on your learnings; they won't necessarily be the ones to act on the feedback, but they'll need to be aware, and they'll need to assign resources within their departments to make any changes or to incorporate the feedback into existing processes or initiatives. They will then need to brief their direct reports so that the insights flow into the hands of the people who will use them.
4. During **team or department meetings**, tell a story about the customer; highlight the insights and how what you learned currently impacts the customer and her ability to complete some job or task.

5. Hold regularly-scheduled department, cross-department, or company **meetings, brown bag lunches, or town halls** to share insights, tell customer stories, answer questions, brainstorm on how to use the insights, etc.

6. Create a **customer room** and share information there—not just the foundational elements (feedback, personas, journey maps) but also the insights, i.e., what does it all mean, for whom, and how should it be operationalized? Ensure that employees can access this room and the information 24/7— maybe it's a virtual customer room.

7. Share the insights during **onboarding, training, and coaching** so that employees understand your customers and know what to expect and what is expected of them (in delivering the experience or in helping to design a better experience).
   - Develop storyboards (or use journey maps) to depict the before and after, to tell the story of the data and of the new, desired outcome/experience.

8. Post feedback and customer comments on **posters** and/or **monitors around the office**. Be sure to provide context for employee clarification and understanding.

9. Develop **videos (or a video series** on a predictable cadence so people come to expect them) to explain what you've learned, what it means, what needs to be done, and by whom. Share these videos in meetings, on monitors, via email communications, in the customer room, during onboarding, and more.

10. Share **customer personas** around the office as well to give employees a better understanding of who your customers are.

11. You could also share pictures of actual customers and share information about who they are, what they do, how they use your products, etc.

Be sure to develop a communication plan that includes ways to best communicate within your organization. (More on that in Chapter 13.) Not all socialization methods work the same in every company; figure out what works best for your company, i.e., what gets executives and employees alike to pay attention and, ultimately and most importantly, take action.

Keep in mind that socializing the insights isn't enough. You need to ensure that the recipients know how to use them or what to do with them.

One parting, but important, thought for this chapter: customer feedback and insights must be engrained into the company's culture, into its DNA; when the customer's perspective becomes not only desired by—but also persuasive—throughout the organization, you have achieved a customer-centric culture.

What gets talked about in an organization and how it gets talked about determines what's going to happen or isn't going to happen. – Susan Scott

11 ACTION PLANNING

"A strategy, even a great one, doesn't implement itself." –
Unknown

Just because you've socialized the insights doesn't mean you're
done. At this point, they are still insights waiting for action. To
move from insights to action, conduct an action planning workshop
at the tactical and strategic levels. Help everyone see how they can
take the data from insights to action to advantage. Help the various
data owners see how they can do something with the data and
insights before them. You're going to have to partner with them—
and spoon-feed them. This is the only way to ensure that the issues
are fixed (at least until this customer-centric mindset becomes the
new norm for everyone).

Action planning is a collaborative process during which
companies address an identified root cause or issue, outline actions
to be taken, and assign ownership, responsibility, and
accountability for each action, ultimately driving toward some
desired outcome, e.g., transforming the experience for the
customer.

Why action planning? Customer listening efforts often end with
closed-loop processes and service recovery efforts that are tactical
at best. These are good first steps, but many times what is really

needed is an overhaul of policies, processes, and infrastructure. Real customer experience transformations require organization-wide adoption and execution of strategic initiatives that lead to meaningful change.

Action planning unites teams, departments, and ultimately, the organization as it allows for cross-functional collaboration to ensure that the next best actions uncovered through their data analysis are prioritized, operationalized, and tracked over time.

Your analytics tools identify actions to take, but often users become stuck and wonder, *"Now what?" "What next?" "How do I fix this?" "Who fixes it?"* Action planning helps managers dig for root causes, assign ownership, and make the improvements necessary to achieve desired outcomes.

Action planning is a collaborative process, as noted earlier. Invite cross-functional stakeholders to participate. It will be important to have that cross-functional representation because you'll partner with stakeholders and shore up those working relationships, bring in some "outside" perspectives, and work toward connecting or breaking down silos, which can inhibit any progress you hope to make. Also, oftentimes, the affected department is too close to the issue; while other departments may not know the issue as intimately, they will bring in other perspectives that open the minds of those most-immediately impacted, especially when it comes to ideation.

You'll also involve key frontline staff in the process, especially those with relevant experience to the improvement area. They are more familiar with the day-to-day processes and interactions than back-office and managerial staff. And they've heard from customers, so they can bring the customer voice and pain points into the discussions.

You may want to include some customers and get their perspectives on the root cause analysis; it's their issue too, and perhaps understanding better what they were trying to do and exactly how they were doing it will provide some insights into the root cause and how it needs to be improved. At the very least, ensure their voice is heard through their feedback; bring feedback, especially verbatims, into these discussions.

You should also involve teams from your governance structure at a high level. They can:

- Make sure that action plans and roadmaps get created.
- Hold teams responsible and accountable.
- Provide oversight and monitoring in order to help drive the projects outlined in the action plans and roadmaps to completion.
- Design and implement a measurement program to evaluate and to measure the customer's experience after improvements are made.
- Educate the organization on the why behind the improvement efforts.
- Communicate progress against the plans to their respective departments.
- Share outcomes with executives and the entire organization.

There are various approaches to action planning, but they ought to all ultimately identify and outline:

- The issue/improvement area
- The root cause
- The intended outcome
- Steps to achieve the outcome
- Feasibility and impact
- Ownership/accountability
- Goal dates
- Success metrics

Gather your collaborators associated with the improvement area to work together to develop a plan for the corrective actions.

***

The first step you'll take is to conduct a root cause analysis of the issue to get to the heart of what needs to be fixed. One of the approaches used for root cause analysis is the **5 Whys**, known for its simplistic nature, i.e., easy to explain and to understand. But don't let its simplicity fool you; it works.

> *"5 Whys is an iterative, interrogative technique used to explore the cause-and-effect relationships underlying a particular problem. The primary goal of the technique is to determine the root cause of a defect or problem by repeating the question "Why?" Each question forms the basis of the next question. The "5" in the name derives from an anecdotal observation on the number of iterations needed to resolve the problem."*

Simply state the problem, and then ask "*Why?*" five times to drill down to the ultimate cause. Don't focus on symptoms of the problem, focus on causes. You can adapt this process to your needs; sometimes asking "*Why?*" five times is too many, and sometimes, you need to ask it more than five times.

An example that is often cited is Jeff Bezos using 5 Whys to understand why an employee was injured on the job at Amazon. (In this example, he only asks "*Why?*" four times, which happens, to get to the root cause.)

Why did the associate damage his thumb?
Because his thumb got caught in the conveyor.

Why did his thumb get caught in the conveyor?
Because he was chasing his bag, which was on a running conveyor belt.

Why did he chase his bag?
Because he placed his bag on the conveyor, but it then turned on by surprise.

Why was his bag on the conveyor?
Because he used the conveyor as a table.

As you can see, the root of the problem is that there was no place for the employee to store his bag. But you may also find that different people in the exercise go down different paths, which may result in the same root cause—or they may find yet another cause (or root cause, which you must determine).

Use an Action Planning Template like the one below to research and document your plan, or develop something similar.

ACTION PLANNING TEMPLATE

Problem Statement	Root Cause	Actions to be Taken	Desired Customer Outcome
What is the problem to be resolved and experience to be redesigned? What is the current experience for the customer? What are customers saying about this issue?	Conduct 5 Whys to determine the root cause.	What are the actions to be taken to fix the root cause?	Once the root cause is resolved, the new customer experience will be: xxx. We want customers to: [do] We want customers to: [think/goal] We want customers to: [feel]
Owner	**Approver**	**Other Resources**	**Desired Business Outcome**
Who sees this project through to completion and is responsible for all of the moving parts?	Which executive(s) needs to approve the project and the budget?	Who else will be involved in resolving and redesigning this problem area?	Once the root cause is resolved, the new customer experience will mean X for the business.
Customer Impact	**Cost to Fix**	**Time to Fix**	**Revenue Impact**
How does this solve the problem for them? Potential increase in CX metrics? Number/percent of customers impacted?			H/M/L or % increase
Feasibility	**Priority**	**Completion Date**	**Success Metrics**
H/M/L based on internal criteria	Relative to other initiatives	Link project plan to this document	How will you know you've successfully completed the project and designed a better experience for your customers?

At a high level, here's the flow of the template.

Once you've identified the root cause, you can then outline the intended outcome, i.e., what the corrected process should look like. Then, you'll brainstorm ideas on how to resolve the root cause and achieve the outcome. That ideation is important because not every idea is feasible from a timing, cost, or resource perspective, yet they should all be explored.

For each solution/idea, assign a feasibility rating based on cost to fix, time to fix, resources to fix (including availability), impact on customer, and impact on revenues. Prioritize each idea based on that rating and relative to other solutions for other issues/change initiatives. Select the "winning" idea and assign ownership and accountability.

Next, the owner will outline a step-by-step corrective plan, or strategic roadmap, that spells out exactly how the solution will be executed, when, and with which specific resources (human, financial, and other). A budget will be developed and needs to be reviewed and approved by the executive committee before the team can move forward with executing the plan. Outcomes need to be stated and clarified.

What's next?

Let's assume you've received executive approval to forge ahead. Congratulations!

Now the work begins. It's time to execute. Create a project plan with clear steps, timelines, and ownership assignments. Progress touchpoints and success metrics need to be identified. And a final deadline must be established.

Rally the troops, and go do it. Implement the changes, test them with customers, and modify as needed. Educate employees on new tools or processes, and communicate to customers about the changes that were made. Close the loop with all essential parties.

As changes are being implemented, the governance team ought to provide oversight. Employees will need to be held accountable for their assigned parts and pieces. And it will be necessary to measure the impact of the improvements on both the customer and the business.

In the end, just listening to customers or just saying that you've got data is meaningless. Uncovering insights and not doing anything with them is sinful. Customer experience is the most powerful business differentiator today, but as you know, transforming the customer experience is a lot of work. Listening to customers is only half the battle. Doing something with what you've heard wins the battle.

Don't get stuck focusing on the numbers. Customers are telling you what you need to do to earn or to keep their business. Do it. Use their feedback to transform the experience and to help them solve the problems they are trying to solve; the numbers will follow.

When you hear me during workshops or keynotes, or when you read in my blogs or articles, about going from data to insights to advantage, that's the advantage: **You did the work that no one else did or wants to do. And guess what? You achieved the outcomes that no one else did! Advantage you!**

The first step in exceeding your customer's expectations is to know those expectations. –Roy H. Williams

ENDNOTES
Source for 5 Whys definition: "Five Whys Technique," adb.org. Asian Development Bank. February 2009. Retrieved 26 March 2012.

Annette Franz

12 OUTCOMES

That's a good segue into talking about outcomes.

What are outcomes? They're basically the result—or the consequence—of something, of doing something.

In our case, outcomes are the result of putting forth all of this effort to improve the customer experience. It takes time and effort to achieve these outcomes, and any work (including the effort and the resources—financial, human, capital, or other) that you put into designing and delivering a new and better experience should be linked to the desired outcome.

As with any other work or project or initiative (although this customer experience transformation is not any of those!), you've got to start with the end in mind. What's the objective, and what's the desired outcome?

Outcomes should be defined for the business and for the customer and employee. Some examples of outcomes for each, some of which I've mentioned earlier in the book, include:

Business
- Increased revenue: from new customers, existing customers making additional purchases, and existing customers deepening their relationships by expanding to other

product lines (reduced churn, increased retention, increased brand preference, stronger customer relationships)
- Provider and employer of choice
- Reduced costs: often in the form of process efficiencies and improvements (reduced/shorter sales cycles)
- Culture change: a shift to a people-first culture
- Increased referrals: as a result of an improved experience, which also yields reduced sales and marketing costs
- Create and deliver customer value: through customer-centric features and product enhancements, customer-centric product ideas
- Innovation: innovative products and experience
- Greater shareholder returns

Customers
- Achieved a job to be done
- Solved a pain point
- Reduced effort or simplified interaction/transaction
- Memorable experience
- Received value

Employees
- Career growth and development
- Got a promotion
- Increased job satisfaction
- Expectations met
- Great experience

Note that these things cannot be achieved without taking real action on your feedback. And you must link actions to outcomes.

Desired outcomes must be measurable, else how will you know you've achieved them if you haven't devised a way to measure success? Success metrics might include:

Business
- ROI
- Cost savings

- Revenue
- Retention
- Customer lifetime value (CLV)

Customer
- Net promoter score (NPS)
- Customer satisfaction (CSAT)
- Customer effort score (CES)
- Expectations met
- First call resolution (FCR)

Employee
- Employee engagement
- Employee satisfaction
- % Ownership of customer issues
- % Employees know who your customers are
- % Employees who know key drivers of customer experience

When you take the time to understand your customers, and when you use those understandings to intentionally design an experience that your customers desire—an experience that gets them to buy, buy more, or buy again—then you will achieve the outcomes you intended.

The right actions undertaken for the right reasons generally lead to good outcomes over time. –John Mackey

Annette Franz

13 COMMUNICATION PLANNING

Congratulations! You've done the work. (You are going to, right?!) You are way ahead of the pack. There are still so many companies just sitting on the data, paralyzed by the possibilities.

I wrote earlier about socializing the data and insights. Another important aspect is to communicate to employees and to customers what you're doing, why you're doing it, and what's next.

I thought I'd pause here before I delve into the next section on the second customer understanding tool, Characterize, and talk about, well, talking about it—communicating the work you're doing. This is important for a variety of reasons, so let me start there.

There are different types of communications that are used, obviously, for different reasons. They include:

- **Explanatory**: Answer questions every constituency will have about the work that you are doing. Answers the 5 W's and the H (who, what, when, where, why, and how).
- **Persuasive**: Inspiring or motivating your audience to commit, adopt, adapt, or change.
- **Informational**: Provide updates and information about the work that you're doing.
- **Closed-loop**: Share with employees and customers what

has been done with their feedback; share customer feedback with employees.

- **Coaching**: Use customer and employee feedback to improve employee performance.
- **Training**: Teach employees about how to use the new processes or systems and how to deliver the new experience.
- **Rewards and recognition**: Yes, this is a type of communication too. Appreciate employees for delighting customers and for doing a great job. Celebrate successes.

Obviously, the first thing to know when it comes to communications is your audience. Knowing who the audience is guides the message and the delivery.

Let's start with your first audience, employees. What do they want to know about this customer experience transformation work? Here are some questions you'll need to answer for them:

- What is it? What's changing?
- Why is it changing?
- How long will it take?
- What's the impact on the business?
- What does it mean for me?
- What's my role?
- How can I get involved?
- What's in it for me?
- What happens if I don't get involved?
- What happens if I don't change?
- What happens if we (company) don't change?

What about customers? What do they want to know? Here are some questions to answer for them:

- What is it? What's changing?
- What will it look like after its changed?
- Why is it changing?
- How long will it take?
- How will it impact me? Our relationship?
- How will you keep me in the loop?

- What do you need from me?
- If I provide feedback, what will you do with it?

The contents of your communications should be simple, relevant, consistent, motivational—and the communications should be ongoing to create awareness and to inspire and educate.

There's a lot to think about here, and they'll likely ask more questions, but here are some content ideas:

- Explain the areas of focus for your transformation
- Share the customer experience vision, the change vision, and especially, the desired outcomes
- Talk about employee listening
- Talk about customer listening and share feedback
- Explain what has already been done
- Outline the next three months—and then give it to them in bite-sized chunks over time after the initial communication
- Provide progress on each milestone as you go along
- Share quick wins and improvements made (and train as needed)
- Talk about metrics, dashboards—tracking success
- Answer questions on the previous page for each constituency
- Link back to company values, as much as possible

And as much as possible, you've got to involve the employees in this work. I already talked about your governance structure and activating and driving lasting change. You've got to do all of that—and do it right.

I'm often asked about different methods or channels to use to communicate with employees because, for shame, they don't read your emails! Here are some suggested alternative internal modes of communication:

- Brown bag lunches
- Videos/video series
- Employee, customer newsletters

- Orientation, onboarding, training, coaching
- Rewards and recognition
- Modeled behavior/roleplaying
- Company intranet, including an FAQ page
- Customer room
- Journey maps
- Company meetings, 1:1 meetings

Don't expect to communicate on a whim. You've got to have a plan in place that outlines the various communication needs for your customer experience work. That plan must be coordinated with other HR and Marketing messaging to the respective recipients (employees and customers). You've got to develop a communication plan and then link it—or fold it into—the HR and Marketing communication plans.

CX COMMUNICATION PLAN					
WHAT	WHY	FROM WHOM	TO WHOM	HOW	WHEN

Ideally, the plan becomes centralized. You should be working in partnership with various stakeholders around the organization who need to communicate to employees and customers on a regular basis to ensure there isn't overlap or confusion. Put forth a cohesive and coordinated effort. Know this: communications are often the most overlooked part of the experience.

The conversation is the relationship. If the conversation stops, so does the relationship. –Susan Scott

CHARACTERIZE

14 CHARACTERIZE CUSTOMERS

The second approach to achieving customer understanding—and the second way to put the "customer" in *customer* experience—is to characterize your customers. This approach is all about developing customer personas.

Who are your customers? Do you *really* know who your customers are? Do you know what their goals and desired outcomes are? Do you know what problems they are trying to solve? And what jobs they are trying to do?

How does your company define or segment customers? Do you talk about "profiles" or "target segments" or "target customers" or "target demographics?" Guess what? Your customers are not "target anything." If you think your customers are men between the ages of 18 and 49, for example, you're dead wrong.

When it comes to understanding who customers are, what their needs are, what they're trying to do/achieve with your organization, and how you'll design a better experience, good luck with that! Targets are too broad, high level, ill-defined, and meaningless when it comes to customer experience innovation and design; they don't provide details about needs, goals, attitudes, behaviors, or emotions, and they are just too far from reality and from what the customer is actually doing or trying to do.

You can't take a 30,000-foot view of your customers, which is what targets do, and expect to understand the customer and the current experience, and then design a new and memorable experience. No, there's a better way to describe your prospects or customers. You need to drill down deeper and develop personas, which will focus on the needs and jobs to be done by the customer.

What are Personas?

Personas are descriptions that represent a behavioral grouping of customers and are specific to your business, not to the industry. The descriptions include vivid narratives, images, and other items that help companies understand who their customers are, understand the needs of the customer (contextual insights), and outline motivations, goals, behaviors, challenges, likes, dislikes, objections, and interests that drive buying (or other) decisions.

Personas are up close and personal—literally. Personas are fictional characters or characterizations you create to represent the various types of customers that (might) buy from you or that use your products or services.

How Do I Develop Personas?

Personas are derived through primary research (interviews, surveys, ethnographic research)—research that can then also be used in your customer journey maps—and can also include existing behavioral (interaction, transaction) data to develop a complete picture.

Let me just take a moment to note here that you must conduct the research. Do the work. Don't develop personas by gathering a group of employees and creating assumptive personas or compiling persona descriptions based on what you *think* you know about your customers. This perpetuates inside-out thinking. It's not accurate. And it's lazy. Customer understanding is rooted in talking to your customers, so go talk to your customers!

The primary research you conduct will allow you to learn more about the customer: his needs, goals, behaviors, demographics, motivations, problems to solve, etc. Importantly, you are trying to understand what jobs customers are trying to do, what problems they are trying to solve. Each persona is then described in detail based on the unique characteristics that comprise it.

And let's not forget that each persona includes a human face and name. Doing so humanizes the persona and further helps to make him/her relatable and personal, while at the same time building awareness and empathy. Big Lots, an American discount retailer, has a persona named Jennifer that has been referenced regularly by Big Lots' CEO during analyst calls.

Personas are living, breathing artifacts. They must be updated because customers change, and the business evolves. As this happens, you may find yourself adding new personas as well.

Why Use Personas?

Using personas to define your customers allows you to shift from target-thinking and broad-based thinking about your customers to a more actionable definition or view. If you really want to develop a personalized experience for your customers, your first step is to do your homework and develop personas. Personas take you one step closer to a customer-driven transformation.

Personas are actionable; once you understand who your customers are, you are better able to create and target messaging, design products and services, and deliver a more relevant experience, on top of which you can layer personalization.

Personas also:

- Shift the organization's focus outside in (on the customer), as it should be, rather than inside out
- Really put the experience in the customer's perspective and make you think about the customer as a "real human"
- Help everyone understand who the customer is and obsess about the customer's needs
- And keep people from forming their own opinions about who the customer really is—everyone is on the same page
- Get everyone speaking the same language about your customers

- Develop empathy for the customer
- Bring the customer to life
- Shift "target demographic" thinking to a more actionable definition/view of customers
  - Targets don't provide details about needs, goals, attitudes, behaviors, emotions
  - Targets are too far from reality
- Drive engagement and ongoing understanding of the customer, especially since they need to be reviewed and updated on a regular basis

How to Assign Personas?

You will likely want to assign personas to prospects and customers. How might you do that? There are a couple of approaches that are most effective, all embracing self-selection:

- When prospects or customers complete a form online, ask a clarifying question (e.g., "I am best described as . . ."—but don't actually use persona names there; use descriptors instead) that would then allow you to assign them with a persona.
- When you're talking to a prospect or customer on the phone, ask the same or similar clarifying question(s) so that you can assign a persona to them.
- Note that when you're recruiting customers of certain persona types for journey mapping workshops, which I'll write more about in an upcoming chapter, you can ask (and capture the response to) the clarifying or identifying question(s) as part of your recruiting screener.

Different Types of Personas

Many people don't realize that there are different types of personas. Know this: as a customer experience professional, you are most interested in *design personas*. Let's take a look at the difference between marketing personas and design personas.

Marketing personas include details such as demographics, brand preferences, why they shop, how they shop, motivations, buying power, personalities, etc. They are typically used by marketers for lead-generation purposes to identify who potential buyers are and how to best market to them. They help marketers plan offers and content that align to their prospects' and customers' preferences. (And yes, this is part of the overall experience!)

Design personas, on the other hand, include details about needs, pain points, problems to solve, jobs to be done, goals, desired outcomes, feelings, feedback from voice of the customer programs, etc. (They will also include some of the other details found in marketing personas.) They help to keep you from injecting your own assumptions about who the customer is and what she is trying to achieve, build empathy for the customer, and are used to design products, services, and the experience. They remind designers who they are designing for and what's important to the customer.

Know that personas can be developed for both B2C and B2B customers. B2B personas might contain some demographics and firmographics, but probably, the largest difference is that these often tend to be role-based. As you can imagine, different roles within an organization have different goals, problems to solve, and jobs to be done. But don't stop there; do the research to understand those goals, problems to solve, pain points, etc.

If your marketing department has already developed personas for their purposes, you can take those and then layer an empathy map on top of them. This will take what you already know, layer on some additional research and data, and allow you to present the customer in a more empathetic way.

Empathy Maps

What is an empathy map? It is not the same thing as a persona, and it is not the same as a journey map. (Yes, someone actually asked me if empathy maps and journey maps are one and the same.) Here's what empathy maps are, straight from the creator's mouth:

> Empathy maps *"help teams develop deep, shared understanding and empathy for other people. People use it to help them improve customer experience, to navigate organizational politics, to design better work environments, and a host of other things. The*

empathy map was created with a pretty specific set of ideas and is designed as a framework to complement an exercise in developing empathy." (Dave Gray, Founder, XPLANE)

The image below is Dave's updated version of an empathy map canvas. You can download it at: gamestorming.com/empathy-map-canvas-006/.

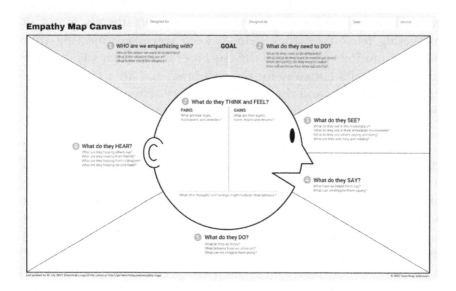

I'm not going to take the time in this book to define in detail how to create personas or empathy maps. Know that the process is more complex than gathering a bunch of people in a room to answer the questions you need answered in order to develop a persona. The persona development process requires a bit of heavy lifting, and if (when, i.e., do this!) you hire a research firm to do the work for you, it could be a six-figure project, easily.

But I needed to devote a little bit of time explaining what they are because they are the second customer understanding tool—they are the "understand who your customers are" part of the equation. And you need to know what they are and why you need to use them; they'll be an integral part of designing a better experience for your customers.

Where to Use Personas

Personas and empathy maps bring you (and your employees) closer to the customer, help you understand the customer, and develop empathy for the customer. There are several ways you'll use personas in your customer experience work, including:

- Socialize them throughout the organization to give employees a solid awareness and understanding of who your customers really are and what they expect.
- Use them as a starting point to develop new products, services, apps, or websites.
- They become the characters in your journey mapping stories; they help to build empathy for the customer for whom you are mapping and bring understanding of the customer.
- Frame your messaging and outreach based on personas to ensure the appropriate content and channels are being used.

Persona Observations

There are a couple of interesting observations I've made about personas in the last few years:

- Not every company has developed personas.
- For those who have, they are usually developed, owned, and used by only one group.
- For those with personas, some haven't done the research to develop them; they're purely assumptive personas.
- Personas are typically created based on the buyer funnel or for the sole purpose of marketing and selling products and services.
- Many customer experience professionals don't know that they should be starting customer understanding and customer experience design with personas.
- For those who do know they should do this, many don't understand the difference between marketing personas and design personas.
- Or they don't even know that they should be using design personas, not marketing personas.

Do this: find out if personas have been created in your organization. Not sure where to look/ask? Start with marketing, and then head over to your UX team. If marketing doesn't have them, UX will, for sure.

If you don't find any personas, you need to develop them; if you find them, make sure they fit your needs of CX design.

You're going to need personas as we dive into the next section on journey mapping. If the ones you've found are buyer personas, you're going to need to do a bit more homework to develop the design personas. At the very least, layer an empathy map on top of what you already know about the existing personas. That will take you closer to who the customer really is. Be sure to test and validate with customers after you've layered on the empathy map.

Empathy is seeing with the eyes of another, listening with the ears of another, and feeling with the heart of another. –Alfred Adler

ENDNOTES
Source for Big Lots persona: https://blogs.wsj.com/corporate-intelligence/2013/08/30/jennifer-oh-jenny-why-a-large-company-is-focused-on-one-lady/
Source for empathy map definition and graphic: https://medium.com/the-xplane-collection/updated-empathy-map-canvas-46df22df3c8a

EMPATHIZE

15 EMPATHIZE WITH CUSTOMERS

The final approach to achieving customer understanding—and to putting the "customer" in *customer* experience—is to empathize with your customers. There is no better way to do this than to walk in their shoes, to experience what they experience when interacting with your brand. I'm talking about journey mapping. I'll go into more detailed definitions in a minute, but let's start with why you need to map the customer experience.

Why Map Customer Journeys

Journey mapping is a learning exercise. Companies learn about their customers and about the experience they put them through to interact with the business. And that learning allows them to become more customer-centric and more aware of the experiences they create for their customers. That's just the beginning. Done right, map customer journeys to:

- **Understand the experience today**: maps bring understanding and identify what customers do, think, and feel as they interact with your brand; they highlight and help diagnose existing issues and opportunities. Don't forget that they capture what's going well too.
- **Evaluate current experiences**: the maps allow you to measure, highlight, and diagnose existing issues and opportunities.
- **Design new experiences for tomorrow**: the maps force

you to prioritize and rethink existing processes, products, or services and/or create new ones.

- **Implement and activate new experiences**: the future-state maps become the blueprints or statements of direction for the work to be done to improve the experience.
- **Inform your CX strategy**: the maps will help you identify listening gaps, improvement opportunities, and operational (in)efficiencies.
- **Communicate and socialize experiences**: use the maps to tell the customer's story during onboarding, training, and other ongoing education opportunities to unite the organization around the customer, to teach employees about the current and the future experience, and to further ingrain the customer-focused culture of the business
- **Align the organization around the customer**: maps are great tools to get executive commitment for your customer experience transformation, get organizational adoption of the customer-centric focus, provide a line of sight to the customer for employees, and help employees understand how they impact the experience.
- **Shift the organizational culture and mindset in two ways**: 1. *From inside out to outside in*: maps are created by customers, from the customer viewpoint; bringing their voice into the organization is the first step toward shifting that mindset. 2. *From touchpoints to journeys*: maps help you think about the entire customer journey, the entire relationship with the organization; realize that journey thinking means to consider both what happened prior to the interaction that you're mapping and what the customer will do next.

These sound like lofty goals and outcomes, but if you've been through the mapping process and have done it correctly, you know this isn't a stretch.

Need some proof that journey mapping really is all that? Did you hear about the Macy's turnaround story in 2018? Jeffrey Gennette, Macy's CEO, credited journey mapping as the foundation of the turnaround. Sadly, at the time that this book is being published,

Macy's has taken a major hit again and is facing a downturn. I suspect it's partially because Macy's didn't embrace the entire mapping process. You can't just map, make some cosmetic fixes, and call it a day; there's so much more to it than that. Keep reading!

***

Let's move on to some definitions.

Journey Mapping—Current State

Journey mapping is a creative process in which you illustrate—with customers—the steps they take for some interaction they had with your company, some journey they were taking to complete a task and to achieve a desired outcome. It's a timeline of what customers are doing, thinking, and feeling throughout the experience. The map tells the story of the customer's journey as she interacts with your brand, all the while building empathy for her. Once companies understand how they make the customer feel, they can identify gaps in the journey and areas for improvement, fix the pain points, and ensure they keep delivering on the delighters.

Journey Mapping—Future State

In future-state journey mapping, you ideate—with customers—the ideal future experience and map out that experience, which then becomes the blueprint for implementation. The future-state map shows what the customer *will* be doing, thinking, and feeling (in the future ideal experience) throughout the respective interactions with the brand.

This table clarifies differences between current-state and future-state maps.

CURRENT STATE MAP	FUTURE STATE MAP
Understand today's experience	Design tomorrow's experience
Is grounded in data	Is rooted in creativity and ideals
Identifies pain points/high points	Ideate solutions for pain points
Identifies listening gaps	Incorporate listening posts, as needed
Identifies incremental improvements	Communicates and is driven by CX vision
Identifies opportunities to deliver value	Used to design/deliver new value, products, services

Always start with mapping the current state. You can't transform something you don't understand. Start by understanding the good and the bad of the current experience.

Know this: journey mapping is a tool and a process. Just because you've created the map doesn't mean you're done. There's still a lot of work to do. That work yields some amazing outcomes for your company and for your customers. More on that in a bit.

Assumptive Mapping
You are assumptive mapping when you gather a group of stakeholders in a room and map the customer journey based on what *you think* the experience is—based on feedback, your own experience, etc. You are *assuming* you know what the experience is. Starting with an assumptive map is not wrong, but if you do so, you must validate with customers, which many companies don't do. Unfortunately, most assumptive mapping is actually process mapping in disguise!

Lifecycle Mapping
Lifecycle mapping is the process of creating a map that shows all of the phases of the customer's relationship with your company. It's high level and is important for understanding the customer's overall relationship with the organization, from before he's a customer through when he terminates the relationship. It typically includes these stages: Need, Awareness, Consideration, Selection/Purchase, Experience, Loyalty, Advocacy, Engagement, Raving Fans, and Exit. It's not linear and often circles back on itself.

Touchpoint Mapping
In touchpoint mapping, you create a master map that outlines all of the stages of the experience or of the lifecycle with the brand, and then capture every touchpoint and interaction the customer has within each stage. You interview customers and stakeholders to identify all of the points of contact that the customer has with the brand within each stage. Touchpoint maps are also great vehicles to capture and inventory your current listening posts, identify painful touchpoints based on customer feedback, identify friction and leakage points, and identify listening gaps at a high level. (Refer back to Chapter 7 for more details on the feedback map.) Based on

this information, the next step is to map the journey to and through the painful or problematic touchpoints.

Touchpoint

Touchpoints are any method or way that a customer comes into contact with or interacts with a brand, or vice versa, that might impact the way the customer feels about the brand. Some touchpoints, such as online reviews that are not initiated by the brand, may be outside of the brand's control.

Moments of Truth

Moments of truth are those make-or-break moments in the experience the customer expects you to execute flawlessly; if you don't, she may not continue with the transaction or interaction—or with the relationship. But when executed flawlessly, the moment delights the customer, assuring her that it's the right decision to continue with the transaction and with the relationship. They are moments that cause customers to form impressions of your brand and, as a result, become a decision point for them.

Interactions

Sometimes person to person, sometimes person to system—it's how the customer engages with the brand and vice versa. Channels are where the interactions take place. Interactions are what happen at the touchpoint.

Service Blueprint

This is a new concept for many folks, but it's not a new concept at all. If you're journey mapping (correctly) but haven't created a service blueprint, you're using journey mapping the tool, not journey mapping the process. And you're probably not making/seeing any improvements in the experience.

While the journey map provides an end-to-end view of the customer experience, the service blueprint provides a customer-to-core view. It is a behind-the-scenes look at the people, tools, systems, policies, and processes that support and facilitate the experience you've mapped. It also includes people, tools, and systems that your customers have interacted with during their experience. More on this later.

Process Mapping

During process mapping, you document the internal workflow that supports the experience that the customer is having. Process mapping is important and needs to be done, but it is all about what's happening internally. It has nothing to do with the customer's perspective, although your internal processes certainly can, and will, impact the customer experience.

Value-Stream Mapping

According to Wikipedia:

"Value-stream mapping is a lean-management method for analyzing the current state and designing a future state for the series of events that take a product or service from its beginning through to the customer with reduced lean wastes as compared to current map. A value stream focuses on areas of a firm that add value to a product or service, whereas a value chain refers to all of the activities within a company. The purpose of value-stream mapping is to identify and remove or reduce "waste" in value streams, thereby increasing the efficiency of a given value stream. Waste removal is intended to increase productivity by creating leaner operations, which in turn make waste and quality problems easier to identify."

Value-stream mapping should ultimately be a part of your journey mapping process, working hand in hand with service blueprinting.

***

It's important to understand the definitions and the differences between these map types. Use each one properly and at the appropriate time. That (done properly) is a good segue into the next chapter, in which I debunk the myth that journey mapping is a waste of time.

Nothing ever becomes real 'til it is experienced. –John Keats

ENDNOTES

Source for Macy's turnaround story:
https://www.cio.com/article/3268004/macys-ceo-credits-customer-journey-mapping-as-the-foundation-of-their-turnaround.html

Source for value-stream mapping definition:
https://en.wikipedia.org/wiki/Value-stream_mapping

16 BUT, MAPS ARE A WASTE OF TIME . . .

A few years ago, Esteban Kolsky did some research on journey mapping and uncovered that 34 percent of companies used journey mapping. Of that 34 percent . . .

- 2% of companies reported success
- 13% said it worked for them, and
- 72% said it missed their needs.

Seventy-two percent said it missed their needs! Wow. What's going on there? (By the way, he's not the only one to come to this conclusion; for a while, this—or some variation of this—was the darling headline: "Journey Maps are a Waste of Time.")

I'll tell you what's going on: they're doing it all wrong. They're not really mapping. When you do it right, you can effect real change. Ask (cautiously) the CEO of Macy's about that. Recall that he's the one who publicly acknowledged that customer journey mapping was the foundation of the Macy's turnaround.

I'm often asked to speak about journey mapping or with journey mapping as a piece of the talk, and I've learned, or rather confirmed, a lot. Namely, you might think you're journey mapping; you call it journey mapping; but it's not really journey mapping.

Here's what happens.

I start by asking the audience if they're journey mapping, and a bunch of hands in the room go up. A lot of hands, as a matter of fact.

Then I proceed to explain what journey mapping is, why you must map, how maps are used in a variety of ways, and what the journey mapping process is.

I then ask the question again. *"How many of you are journey mapping?"* No—or very few—hands go up this second time around. What gives?

One of the things I talk about after I ask the question the first time is that if your map has Need, Awareness, Consideration, Selection, etc. as the column headings, and within each column you've specified relevant or corresponding touchpoints or channels, then you're not journey mapping; you're mapping lifecycle stages, and you're touchpoint mapping. (This is typically where the difference in hands up is rooted.)

Journey maps are defined as "walking in your customer's shoes to understand her experience." That means you go step by step by step to depict the journey, to capture the customer's story of the experience, to depict the timeline of steps she took to go from Point A to Point B.

If you've got lifecycle stages and touchpoints mapped, you are definitely not . . .

- Viewing things from the customer's perspective
- Capturing any kind of detail about the experience
- Able to tell where things go right or wrong
- Able to develop the corresponding service blueprint to fix what's happening inside to support the experience
- Understanding what the customer is doing, thinking, and feeling throughout the experience

As a matter of fact, the customer isn't even in those maps.

The second likely culprit of the gap in hands between the first time I ask and the second time is that folks are creating assumptive maps, which are maps visualized by well-meaning stakeholders who believe they understand the experience; they assume they know. And when people create assumptive maps (which aren't wrong but typically aren't done right), a couple of things happen:

- There's a lot of inside-out thinking; in other words, the map is not created from the customer's perspective.
- It's likely that they've actually created a process map.
- The map doesn't get validated with customers.
- The map gets rolled up, stashed under a desk, and goes nowhere from there.

The first scenario (lifecycle/touchpoint mapping) is the one I hear most often. Neither scenario is good. Don't get me wrong; touchpoint mapping is an important exercise. But just know that this is not journey mapping, and this will not help you improve the experience. It's a first step, but it's not the only step. You should inventory and catalog all of your touchpoints along the customer lifecycle—there are more than you can imagine, and unfortunately, too many of them are overlooked when it comes to the customer experience. You must know them all. And then you must move on to mapping the customer experience (of which those touchpoints are a part).

That doesn't explain all of the 72 percent who said journey mapping missed their needs. Let's look at thirteen other reasons I believe maps will fail you.

1. I've mapped; I'm done.

Actually, creating the map is just the beginning. At this point, it's just a picture with a lot of information. I'll state this many times throughout the rest of the book, but: maps are a tool and a process. Know the tool; embrace the process. When you mapped, I'm sure you uncovered some important findings that need to be used to improve the experience! So you're not done. You've really just begun. And by the way, see point #2. Perhaps you did this too.

2. I've mapped the journey myself; I don't need to involve anyone else.

First of all, the most important person in the room when mapping is the customer. You must map with customers.

Second, actionable maps cannot be created in a vacuum. By definition, the mapping process is a collaborative effort that brings customers and stakeholders of the different departments impacted by the journey being mapped together: for discovering, learning, and sharing. This is where maps help to connect or break down silos.

Third, the journey that's being mapped doesn't operate in isolation. So thinking you can develop a map that wasn't done in conjunction with other departments is erroneous. For example, think about a customer service experience. Imagine that the customer is calling about an issue with the product. You think you only need to have the customer service department represented during the mapping session. Wrong. You should also have stakeholders from sales, marketing, product design, and product marketing in the room, listening and learning.

The customer didn't end up calling customer service just because she was having an issue with the product; she was calling because marketing's messaging was off, sales sold the dream, product design designed a flawed product, and/or product marketing wrote incomplete user or installation instructions.

When these functions are involved in the mapping sessions, they can hear the pain inflicted upon the customer! And they begin to understand the interconnectivity of all departments in designing and delivering the experience for the customer. So imagine that they all get together and fix the root cause of the issue that prompted the customer's call, and then watch as customer satisfaction increases while call volume to the call center decreases. Win-win.

3. One map applies to all customers; all customers are the same.

No, all customers are not the same; and one map does not apply to all customers as a result. This is why you must develop personas first so that you can understand who your customers are, what their needs and expectations are, jobs to be done, problems to solve, etc. Once you've developed the personas, you've got to map each journey for your three to five key personas.

4. I don't need personas; I can simply map for major customer segments or target demographics.

Don't use customer segments or target demographics as your basis for whom you're mapping. They are both too high level and not close enough to the customer for whom you're designing. Customer segments and target demographics are great for marketing and advertising, but they are such broad definitions of your customers and don't get at the level of detailed customer understanding that you need to design an experience that personas afford you.

5. Marketing has the same mapping needs as customer experience professionals.

They don't. Marketing typically maps lifecycle stages and maybe the touchpoints within those stages. They're more concerned with the buyer/sales funnel and how to move prospects and customers through that than individual customer interactions and how to improve the experience.

Customer experience professionals need to know how the interactions fit into the big picture to design a better experience, but they map interactions and specific experiences in order to redesign them. They must map at a detailed level so that they can identify what's going well and what's not. Marketing is not looking at that.

6. Buyer personas and CX personas are one and the same.

Marketing and customer experience professionals have different needs when they are developing and using personas. The personas are developed in much the same way, with lots of research, but customer experience professionals' personas have additional information that allows them to better understand customers so that they can design the experience based on: pain points, problems they are trying to solve, jobs to be done, goals, feelings, etc. The customer experience personas also help to build empathy for customers; I haven't seen many buyer personas that do that.

7. It's okay to start with a future-state map.

Once again: You can't transform something you don't understand. How can you design the future state if you don't understand the current state, i.e., what's right or what's wrong? How do you know what to keep doing and what to stop doing/do differently if you don't understand the current experience first. Start with today, and then work toward tomorrow. If you don't know what's wrong, how can you make it right? Take the time to learn what's working and what's not today before you try to design a better tomorrow.

8. I created an assumptive map and am ready to redesign the experience.

Once you've created the assumptive map, you must have the map validated by customers; that's the only way that I'll advocate for you to do assumptive mapping. If you don't validate with customers, you're simply perpetuating inside-out thinking and are on a path to designing an experience that will definitely not meet your customers' needs.

9. I started the map at the first point of contact with/by the customer.

Actually, the experience for the customer starts well before he contacts or interacts with you. You've got to understand and map the things that happened before and after the actual contact or interaction because that's when the experience began for the customer; don't start mapping where your internal processes begin to support the customer. More on this in future chapters, but the things that happen before and after contact impact—and are part of—the customer's overall experience.

10. Journey maps are used only for the customer experience.

Journey maps are not only created for the customer experience but also for any other constituent whose experience you are trying to improve, including: employees, vendors, partners, franchisees, and licensees. The principles provided in this book apply to journey mapping for any constituent. I recommend you use them to improve the experience for the entire ecosystem because, in the end, the employee, customer, partner, and business will benefit.

11. Without a digital mapping platform, I can't even begin to map.

You can start mapping with butcher paper and sticky notes and then transfer the maps to digital after. I typically start my journey mapping sessions with butcher paper and sticky notes because it facilitates that creative process and gets people up out of their chairs, thinking, questioning, collaborating, and talking to each other. It's more of that design-thinking, creative approach.

It's my preferred approach to mapping; but then afterward, you need to digitize the maps so that you can adhere to the principles of mapping (outlined in detail in the next chapter).

12. Data has no place in journey maps.

Data is a must in your journey maps. And because of that, on the heels of #11, it is one of the reasons you must digitize the maps. Data will bring the maps to life and is essential for a variety of reasons, which I'll get into in Chapter 20. Just know that data is an important piece in the mapping process. And by the way, identifying, finding, and sharing the data is another way to help connect or break down silos that hinder the experience.

13. I have no budget/commitment to make changes.

You heard that journey mapping was a cool—even necessary—thing to do to improve the customer experience. It is a very important tool and process in your entire customer experience management strategy. And that means a couple of things: you can't really do it in a meaningful way until you have executive commitment to the overall strategy, as well as commitment for budget and resources to get the work done.

I've heard plenty of folks talk and write about creating a separate strategy for journey mapping, even a separate governance structure for it. Don't do that! This customer experience transformation work is hard enough without duplicating efforts. There is one customer experience strategy, and there is one governance structure. Journey mapping falls within all of that. And that means you can't do anything meaningful until you have executive commitment.

Keep in mind, though, that journey maps can help you build the business case to get that commitment. But don't try to boil the ocean to do that. Use some of your CX budget to map a journey with customers (preferably with the executive in question in the room for some of it), outline the pain points, make some small improvements, show some quick wins, and win over the entire executive team.

If you're going into the journey mapping process to get executive commitment for your customer experience transformation, that's one thing; but if you've got commitment from above yet cannot get the impacted departments to pony up budget and resources to fix the issues, then something has gone wrong. Here are some questions to consider:

- Who identified the issue/experience to be mapped?
- Were stakeholders involved in conversations prior to the journey mapping workshop?
- Did you discuss the impact and the outcomes of the journey you were mapping (with stakeholders)?
- Did you discuss how the findings would be used (with stakeholders)?
- Was there any discussion about priorities, budget, resources, etc. before the workshop was planned/designed?
- Who was involved in the journey mapping workshops? Which stakeholders?
- Did you debrief with the attendees (internal/stakeholders) after the workshop?

No woman/man is an island. And that couldn't be truer than in customer experience transformation work. You've got to partner with the various departments in your organization, and you have to have the right stakeholders involved from the start of this whole journey mapping process. While feedback from customers or employees may have driven the identification of the journey to be mapped, if stakeholders aren't involved, if owners aren't assigned, if there's no plan beforehand for how findings will be used afterward, you're setting yourself up for failure.

Get commitment for resources—human, time, capital, financial, etc.—from the stakeholders before you conduct the journey mapping workshop with customers. Get commitment that they will use the findings to make improvements. Get commitment that they will do the work immediately/in a timely manner. If you haven't done this, don't bother mapping; you're wasting everyone's time.

***

When you hear people saying that maps are a waste of time and maps aren't actionable, you know that something is missing, something hasn't been done correctly. I'm sure there are more mistakes, but these are the ones I typically see or hear about. Don't make these mistakes!

Remember, journey mapping isn't just a tool, it's a process. You've got to do it right so that the maps drive the change you expected they would. More on that in a couple chapters.

First, some rules . . .

The best journeys answer questions that in the beginning you didn't even think to ask. Jeff Johnson

17 THE PRINCIPLES OF JOURNEY MAPPING

Continuing on with the theme of getting you onto the right path with your journey mapping efforts, it's important to understand the following key principles of journey mapping. When you adhere to these seven basic principles of mapping, you can be certain that your maps become the catalyst for change that they were meant to be!

1. Maps must be created from the customer's perspective.
This is probably the most important principle. Remember, we're talking about putting the "customer" in *customer* experience. How can you possibly do this if the customer is not involved or if you're not thinking about and viewing things from the customer's perspective?

2. Maps must be collaborative/collaborated.
To connect or to break down those organizational silos and to get commitment across the organization for the change that must happen, cross-functional collaboration is necessary. This collaboration is a great reminder to the various key stakeholders that the customer experience isn't one dimensional, i.e., just because the customer calls support doesn't mean support is the only department involved in that interaction. This collaboration also facilitates the assignment of owners to the steps in the journey so that you know who to call on when something is broken. (It goes without saying, although I said it in #1: customers are the primary

collaboration partners!)

3. Maps bring the journey to life.

Maps help bring the customer experience to life for the organization so that everyone understands the experience as it's happening today. To achieve and to amplify this, you'll want to add visuals—images, documents, audio, or video—of what the customer is doing, thinking, and feeling. Attach any artifacts to the map at the relevant step or touchpoint to add greater understanding about the customer journey.

4. Maps must allow you to analyze and prioritize touchpoints and improvement opportunities.

Data must be infused into your maps. The more data you bring into the map, into a touchpoint, the better your ability to analyze the journey and to prioritize improvement opportunities. And the better your ability to drive change. When you can analyze your touchpoints, it's more likely that the map will not just sit on the shelf or just hang on the wall and fail to be the catalyst it's supposed to be.

5. Maps must be shared/socialized.

Once a map is created, don't hoard it, and don't shove it under your desk, never to be seen again. It must be communicated and shared throughout the organization in order to tell the customer's story, to get commitment for the experience and its improvements, to educate employees about the customer's experience and how they contribute and impact it, to teach them the new experience to deliver, and more.

6. Maps must be updated.

Journey maps are not one-and-done efforts or projects; instead, they are living, breathing documents. As improvements are made to the experience and as the experience evolves, you need to update your maps to always reflect the latest current state.

7. Maps are the beginning, not the end.

Just because you've mapped doesn't mean you're done; the maps are so much more than just a pretty picture. You must know the tool but embrace the process. I'll write more about the journey mapping process in the next chapter (and throughout the rest of the book), but I'll share some thoughts here on why and how journey maps are just the beginning.

***

Journey mapping is the most critical and pivotal component in any customer experience transformation. An in-depth understanding of the experience today—what's going well and what isn't—is the only way to really drive change going forward. This is what journey maps provide and, hence, why journey maps and the journey mapping process are often called the backbone of customer experience management.

What do I mean by that? Take a look at the diagram on page 119. As you can see from the diagram, journey mapping (the process) informs and supports so many parts of your customer experience strategy that it literally is the backbone; those parts include:

Executive Alignment
- Helps you build the business case and get executive commitment for the work that lies ahead
- Explains the what and the why behind the customer experience today
- Brings them closer to the customer and allows them to walk in customers' shoes
- By opening their eyes and building that commitment, it ensures all executives are aligned on the customer-centric vision—it's the mindset shift, inside out to outside in

Brand Promise
- Helps you communicate, translate, and amplify the brand promise for your employees
- Aligns the experience with the brand promise
- Identifies where the promise is kept or broken
- Teaches employees about—and aligns them with—the brand promise

Organization Adoption and Alignment
- Teaches employees about the customer and the experience
- Provides a clear line of sight for employees to the customer
- Helps employees understand how they contribute to—and impact—the customer and the experience
- Builds empathy for the customer
- Helps create a universal language for employees to talk about the customer

Employee Experience
- Identifies broken or missing tools, resources, policies, or processes that hinder the experience for the employee (and for the customer)
- Helps the organization align training, tools, and resources to customer needs and expectations
- Highlights how and where the employee experience intersects with the customer experience

Customer Understanding
- Helps the organization understand what the customer is doing, thinking, and feeling as she interacts with the brand
- Helps everyone understand who the customer is and identifies her needs, expectations, preferences, and jobs to be done
- Identifies listening gaps and provides co-creation opportunities with customers
- Identifies key moments of truth (when enriched with data)

Process Improvements
- Becomes the root cause analysis for customer-facing issues
- Identifies operational (in)efficiencies and cost savings
- Is a decision support tool to help prioritize improvement areas
- Facilitates breaking down or connecting organizational silos

The image on the next page helps you visualize how journey maps feed into your customer experience strategy and help you put customers at the center of all you do.

The Backbone of CEM

Journey Maps

Executive Alignment
- Build the business case/get CX commitment
- Explain the what and the why behind customer experience
- Ensure all executives aligned on the customer-centric vision

Org Adoption & Alignment
- Clear line of sight to customer and build empathy for customer
- Understand how they contribute to – and impact – the customer and experience
- Teach employees about customer and experience

Brand Promise
- Communicate and amplify the brand promise
- Identify where promise is kept or broken
- Align employees with the brand promise

Employee Experience
- Align training to customer needs and expectations
- Identify missing/broken tools, resources, processes
- Highlight how the employee experience intersects with the customer experience

Customer Understanding
- Understand what customers are doing, thinking, feeling
- Understand who your customers are, their expectations, and jobs to be done
- Identify listening gaps and provide co-creation opportunities with customers

Process Improvements
- Identify and prioritize key moments of truth/what to fix, what to keep doing
- Identify operational (in)efficiencies and cost savings
- Break down/connect silos

There are many more ways that journey mapping supports and informs your customer experience strategy, including designing new experiences for tomorrow. In Chapter 33, I'll provide details about where you can download a whitepaper I wrote, "30+ Reasons to Map Customer Journeys," which includes more details on this.

When journey mapping is viewed (and used) not only as the process that it is but also, especially, as the backbone of customer experience management, it becomes an ongoing practice and process in your organization. When it becomes part of the conversation, when it feeds into all of the things mentioned on the previous pages (plus the ones in the whitepaper), then it becomes a part of the fabric of the organization.

Are you convinced yet that journey maps are a powerful tool and process in your customer experience toolbox? Good! (I know you answered with a hearty "Yes!")

It's time to move on to the journey mapping process.

Any fool can know. The point is to understand. –Albert Einstein

18 SIX STEPS FROM MAPS TO OUTCOMES

After reading in Chapter 16 what not to do when it comes to journey mapping, I'm sure you're ready for the good stuff, i.e., how to map and what you must do to ensure that the maps are the catalyst for change that they are meant to be.

You've got to know and embrace the process I'm about to outline. Doing so ensures that you are on track to doing journey mapping right.

The process I teach for effective journey mapping has the following six steps:

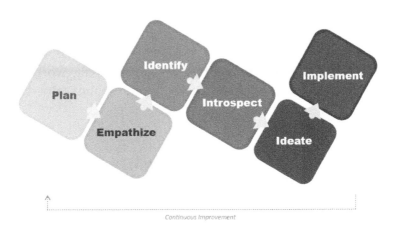

121

You've got to follow the process and use the maps in the ways I'll outline if you want to improve the experience and achieve your desired outcomes.

1. Plan

The first step includes all the prep work to get ready for your workshop, including: identifying the personas for which you'll map; outlining the objectives, scope, outcomes, and success metrics of the map; and identifying the workshop participants.

2. Empathize

The next step is all about the mapping workshop. Map what customers are doing, thinking, and feeling; add data and metrics into the map to help identify moments of truth; bring the map to life with artifacts (e.g., pictures, videos, documents); and assign owners to the customer's steps.

3. Identify

Identify and prioritize moments of truth, research issues, conduct root cause analysis, develop action plans, and assign owners and deadlines to the plan.

4. Introspect

The next step is to look inward by creating a service blueprint and a process map to correspond with the customer journey you've mapped. You can't fix what's happening on the outside, what the customer is experiencing, if you don't fix what's happening behind the scenes.

5. Ideate

In this step, you'll conduct future-state mapping workshops, ideate solutions to customer and backstage pain points, and design the future state.

6. Implement

The last step in the process is to prototype and test the new design—and fail fast; implement the new experience; share the maps and train employees; close the loop with customers; and update maps to reflect the new current experience.

That's the process at a high level. Starting with the next chapter, I'll take you through each of the steps in detail.

***

As you begin your journey mapping work, think about why you want to map. What are the business challenges you're trying to solve for? What are the customer pain points that you've got to fix in order to improve the experience overall? What are your desired outcomes, for the customer and for the business?

I'm often asked how long this process takes. The best answer I can give you is that it varies, or it depends. It varies based on how long it takes to prepare, and then do, each step in the process. And to do the work. That will largely depend on you and your organization's ability to move—and on how fast or how slow you can move!

But you've also got to keep in mind that this is an ongoing process, a continuous improvement cycle. And you're not going to map just one journey and be done. You will likely have hundreds of journeys to map and take through this six-step process; it's your job to prioritize and to make sense of what to do and when.

If you quit on the process, you are quitting on the result. –Idowu Koyenikan

19 STEP ONE: PLAN

So the first step in the journey mapping process is to plan. *"Fail to plan, plan to fail."* This statement is so true for journey mapping!

This might be a good time to address the question, *"Who owns journey mapping?"* Initially, the CX organization owns journey mapping; as mentioned in a previous chapter, it's a powerful tool in their customer understanding toolbox. Over time, your CX Champions, one of your governance structure committees, can be trained to map customer journeys. It's great to empower others to do this work, but ultimately, it should all be a coordinated effort that still gets run/managed through the CX organization to ensure information sharing and to avoid overlap work.

Okay, let's dive into the planning phase and start with your workshop prep. (Later in the book, I'll provide the details behind running your own journey mapping workshop; for now, I'm taking you through the six-step process to get your mind oriented toward this being a process. Know the tool; embrace the process!)

In preparation for the workshop, you're going to need to identify a few different things. I've outlined them all in detail in this chapter to get you off to a great start.

1. Goals, Objectives, Success Metrics
As with any work that you do—customer experience or other—

you've always got to start at the beginning, identifying your goals and objectives, as well as what success looks like and how to measure it—for the customer and for the business. Some questions to consider at this point include:

- Why are you mapping?
- What are your objectives?
- What business problems are you trying to solve?
- What customer problems are you trying to solve?
- What value will the map(s) bring to the organization?
- What are the intended outcomes for the business and for the customer?
- What changes will you make as a result of the findings?
- Is the organization prepared to make changes?
- How will the outputs be applied internally? By whom?
- Who will own the map and its implementation?

2. Map Scope

Next, you must define (and stick to) the scope of the map. Which interaction are you mapping? What's the start point and what's the endpoint, Point A to Point B? You've got to designate these points to keep everyone focused on the task at hand, but then you must also ensure that everyone sticks to this scope.

You may find that customers come to a fork in the road of their journeys, and you've got to decide which tine to map and which one to capture and map later. Capture the one that you don't map in a "parking lot," and map it later.

This is also a good time to reiterate that you must start with the current-state experience.

When selecting which journeys to map, consider the following:

- Low-hanging fruit: known pain points for the customer
  - o   Source: employees, call center, etc.
- Known pain points for the business, e.g., losing customers, abandoned carts, high call volume, etc.
  - o   Source: touchpoint map findings, metrics, etc.

- Important or impactful journeys for customers where brand's performance is less than optimal
  - Source: surveys and other listening posts
- The journey should have a clear Point A and a Point B, i.e., a clear scope or task and a clear start and end.

3. Personas

Determine for which personas you will map. Remember that you're mapping for personas, as I wrote about in Chapter 14, not for target demographics or segments, which are too high level and too far away from the customer for whom you're designing the experience. Different personas have different experiences, need states, preferences, problems to solve, and jobs to be done—so they will each have their own maps.

When selecting the personas for which to map, be sure to include the following:

- Three to five *key* personas, which are typically defined by the 80/20 rule, i.e., 80 percent of your focus or revenue is on these three to five personas.
- Personas that are representative of a large portion of customers, or their behavior/journey is representative of a large portion of customers.
- Outlier personas, which can be defined as "not the usual suspects." You might include these in your mapping work, especially future-state ideation and mapping, to get a different perspective, which will help you design a differentiated experience.

Once you've selected the persona for which to map, tell the story of that persona for everyone in the workshop. Put people in this persona's shoes from the start of the mapping process.

4. Attendees

Next, you've got to determine who will participate in the workshop. Besides the core CX team, there are two attendees or constituents to think about: (1) customers and (2) stakeholders.

Let's start with customers. This seems like a no-brainer, but I've got to call it out here: *customers must participate in the journey mapping exercise, whether in person or virtually.* This is the one untouchable rule of journey mapping: it is by, with, about, and for the customer (where customer is internal, e.g., employee, or external, e.g., customer, partner, vendor, licensee, etc.).

How do you select the customers to participate? This part is pretty easy. They must be representative of the persona for which you chose to map. And they must both know and be relevant to the journey you are mapping.

If you're mapping in person, recruit six to ten customers to participate in the workshop. If you're mapping virtually, depending on the virtual approach, of which there are several, the answer varies. Some virtual examples include:

- If you're mapping virtually via a Zoom or WebEx session where everyone is on video and one person is in charge of placing the sticky notes on the butcher paper, then I'd stick with six to ten customers. (You don't have to capture the map on butcher paper and sticky notes; you can capture it in Google Sheets, where everyone can track with the map as it evolves.)
- If you're mapping virtually via a digital journey mapping platform that doesn't have online community-like capabilities, then you'll want to keep the number low as well.
- If you're mapping virtually via an online community or some variation of that (with synchronous and asynchronous options), recruit no fewer than thirty but ideally closer to one hundred to participate.

Your approach may differ slightly here if you're a B2C company versus B2B. Both can use what I just outlined above. For many B2B companies, I have mapped with the client's customers 1:1; in other words, the journey maps were account-based, not a room full of competitive (or not) customers. My B2B clients have preferred this approach as it allows them to also use the journey mapping workshop (and subsequent follow-up, improvements, etc.) as a relationship-building platform. For the most part, this has worked well and has been successful for both clients and their customers.

One other difference is that, for B2C, you'll offer customers an incentive to participate in the workshop. Be sure to tell customers this during the recruitment process. (You won't be offering incentives to B2B customers, for a variety of reasons, not the least of which is corporate gifting policies.)

The next set of attendees you need to consider and invite are the stakeholders. You want to make sure that you include the right stakeholders in these workshops. If you're mapping a customer service experience, for example, you'll have the head of customer service in the room, but there will be others as well. I recommend including marketing, sales, product design, product marketing, and billing too, depending on if you're mapping a specific type of call/issue.

Why? Because they are the reason the customer is contacting customer service! Because marketing's messaging was off; sales sold the dream; there was a flaw in the product design; the product documentation was inaccurate and not thorough; and/or the invoice was confusing and inaccurate. When these stakeholders hear the issues that customers are having—straight from the horse's (customer's) mouth—they are immediately alerted to how their department impacts the experience, and they are shown how the experience is cross-functional and doesn't just happen in one department. And imagine if they fixed the issues upstream so that the customer never has to call, thus reducing call volume downstream (at the call center). Sounds like some serious cost savings to me.

So think about stakeholder attendees in that way; when you're planning who to invite: be sure to have representatives from the various departments that touch the journeys you'll be mapping. Think upstream and downstream. Make sure attendees have a stake in the game, that they have a vested interest in the journeys being mapped and can advocate for what they learn during the workshop to their departments and the rest of the organization.

If a key stakeholder cannot attend, make sure there's a plan to follow up with him/her immediately after the workshop. And have the stakeholder send an alternate from his/her department, someone who is relevant to, or very familiar with, the journey being mapped.

But note this: *do not have more stakeholders than customers in the room.*

The final attendee in the room should be a note-taker, someone who's meticulous about capturing comments, questions, conversations, etc. If you can record (video or even just audio) the workshop, that's ideal, especially if you've got key folks who can't attend.

I can't end this section without noting that if your CEO can attend any portion of the workshop, especially if you haven't yet gotten full commitment for the customer experience strategy, make it happen. It's eye-opening for everyone, especially the CEO, who is often far-removed from the day-to-day customer interactions. I've witnessed CEOs giving their commitment for the work that lies ahead as a result of witnessing the journey mapping workshop.

5. Attendee Prep Meetings

Once you've identified and recruited your attendees, the next thing you'll need to do is conduct a pre-workshop prep session, one for customers, one for stakeholders. The content of the sessions will be roughly the same for customers and for stakeholders, but you'll be able to talk about the internal workings and next steps with stakeholders.

For the customer pre-workshop prep session, you'll cover:

- What is journey mapping?
- Why are we journey mapping?
- What journeys are we mapping?
- Who am I? What are my needs as the customer? (Don't talk about personas; talk about the customer whose story you're going to unravel or unfold.)

- Why am I participating?
- What are the ground rules?
- What is expected of me? What's my role?
- How do I prepare?
  - Bring notes or journals of the steps that you take to go from point A to point B for the journeys we've selected to map—also think about what happened just before and right after
  - Think about the people, documents, and systems you interact with during the experience
  - Think about your needs, feelings, pain points, what's going well
  - Bring artifacts that tell the story, explain your experience, e.g., invoices, documents, videos, pictures, estimates, etc.

For the stakeholder pre-workshop prep session, you'll go into a little more detail on some of these items, sharing the internal needs and perspectives:

- What is journey mapping?
- Why are we mapping?
- What journeys are we mapping?
  - Scope, objectives, success metrics
- Which personas?
  - Paint the picture of the persona(s)
- Why am I participating?
- What are the ground rules? (More on these in Chapter 27.)
- What is expected of me?
- What is my role?
- Do I need to bring anything?

Okay, now that you've got your plan in place and you've scheduled the workshop, it's time to map! In the next chapter, I'll talk through the next step in the six-step process, Empathize.

In preparing for battle I have always found that plans are useless, but planning is indispensable. –Dwight D. Eisenhower

20 STEP TWO: EMPATHIZE

One of the things that journey maps do is tell the customer's story as she interacts with your brand, building empathy for her plight. Yes, it's a plight. Not many brands can use the word "delight" instead of "plight" at the moment! Let's fix that!

The second step in my six-step journey mapping process is Empathize. This is the step in which we actually map. I'm going to devote a section later in the book (after the six-step process) to teach you how to facilitate your own journey mapping workshop. In this chapter, I'm going to cover high-level concepts of the workshop.

As you run through the workshop, there are many things to do and consider.

First things first. What mapping framework should you use? There are a lot of different ones, but they all (should) have three things that they must capture in common: what the customer is (1) doing, (2) thinking, and (3) feeling. You can add more swim lanes than that to your map, but you must capture these three things—or you're not journey mapping!

Other swim lanes that you can add include what's happening on stage, i.e., what are the tools, systems, documents, and/or people that the customer is interacting with in order to complete the interaction. You might also have a swim lane for channel, timeline (how long the step took), environmental factors, and more.

Don't get hung up in the visualization, either. The map is more than a pretty picture; the story behind it (or that goes into it) is far more important. So be more concerned with the overall mapping process, adhering to the tenets of the process, and how you're going to act on what you learn.

It's important that customers map the experience with as much detail as they can recall. The detail ensures you understand the experience and can more easily identify where things break down. Make sure they map journeys, not lifecycles. Stick to the scope of the map, and ensure they don't stray. If a fork in the road (a micro-journey) is identified, parking lot it for another map/workshop.

Ensure that customers don't problem solve at this point. There will be time to do that when you ideate the future state. Focus on the experience for now. During this step, you are capturing the current state of the experience. Don't lose any ideas; be sure to have a parking lot area set aside for those as well.

Don't process map at this point. This is less likely to happen when customers are mapping, but occasionally, stakeholders in the room want to add their two cents worth and start talking about internal processes. This is not the time. The workshop is all about the customer.

Be sure customers map at the right level of detail so that you really know what's going on. Ask them not to skip steps or to overlook or ignore any detail. The more you can learn about the experience, the more you know, the better equipped you'll be to fix it.

Case in point, customers should map handoffs and things that are outside of your control. You may have to give examples of this from the outset, but that's okay. Again, you want to get the information you'll need to make the right decisions going forward.

An example that I like to use for "things outside of your control" is to think about the experience of going to get coffee. You identify that you need/want coffee. You get in the car and drive to the coffee shop. Traffic is miserable, and there's no parking when you get there.

I just mentioned two steps—traffic and parking—that are outside of your control as the coffee shop owner, but if you were aware of them, you could design the experience to mitigate or to compensate for them. While you have no control over traffic or parking, this is part of the customer's experience, and it ends up reflecting badly on you/your shop.

The customer thinks, *"It's not worth the trip to go there. The coffee is good, but meh, I won't go there again at that hour."* You, as the coffee shop owner, need to create an experience in your store that is traffic worthy! One that has the customer saying, "I'll fight the traffic because I love going there. The coffee is excellent. The service is world-class; they know my name and my drink. The music and the ambiance are relaxing. And I get to play with other people's dogs while I'm reading one of the many magazines and newspapers they offer."

That's a long story to say, do this. Map at that level of detail.

And finally, after the workshop, you'll do three more things to the map: assign owners to each of the steps in the journey; digitize the maps so that you can adhere to the rules of mapping identified in Chapter 17, and add data and metrics into the map, including details about known leakage points, i.e., where you lose customers along the journey, such as shopping cart abandonment.

Assign Owners
You'll need to assign owners to each of the steps in the journey in order to:

- Know who is responsible for fixing what's broken
- Know who to commend for what's going well
- Increase actionability of the map
- Empower change, where needed

- Identify lack of ownership (which could be a problem or the root cause of a problem)
- See how different departments interact and are involved to deliver the experience
- Open the doors to break down and/or connect silos

Digitize the Map

Assuming you created your journey map using butcher paper and sticky notes (as opposed to starting in a digital format), you'll need to move the maps to a digital mapping platform in order to adhere to the rules of mapping.

The rules are as follows. Maps are:

- Created collaboratively, with customers and with other stakeholders
- Shared with the employees who impact the journey that was mapped
- Updated to always reflect the current state of the experience
- Communicated by using them as onboarding and training tools for your organization
- Brought to life with data and artifacts
- Validated by customers, if you started with assumptive maps
- Actionable, meaning they must include enough detail and data to not only truly understand what's going well and what's not but to also be able to identify the moments of truth

Genroe has maintained a nice list of journey mapping platform comparisons, which can be found here:
https://www.genroe.com/blog/journey-mapping-software/11058

Add Data to Maps

The next step, then, is to add data and artifacts into the map. What types of data? Of course, there's a lot of different data to add, but the most important will be from your voice-of-the-customer (VoC) program. Evaluate the available data and determine what's needed, what's most actionable, and incorporate it into the map.

Here's a summary of the different types of data that can be included.

- VoC or customer listening data: reviews, ratings, diagnostics, and verbatims
- Emotions or sentiment data, especially from qualitative sources, e.g., text and voice analytics, sentiment analysis
- Persona data: learnings from your persona research might help you improve the experience or add to the story
- CX metrics: NPS, CSAT, customer effort score, etc.
- Other customer data: interaction, transaction, CLV, reason for call, number of visits to site, where they went on the site, length of site visit, where they exited the site, etc.
- Operational/call center metrics: agent performance, call volume, FCR, hold time, time to resolve, number of transfers, channels used
- Business data: for a lack of a better way to label it, this data is all about the business impact; it's revenue, profitability, retention, cost to fix, time to fix, effort to fix, impact to fix, type of data.
- Artifacts: call recordings, videos, invoices, receipts, pictures, documents, screenshots, etc.

Why do we need to enrich the maps with data? It helps you understand your customers and the experience, make better decisions, and deliver the experience that customers expect. Here are several more reasons for incorporating data into your maps.

Data allows you to:

- Measure the journey—the steps and the overall journey
- More deeply analyze the experience and facilitates understanding
- Identify and clarify high points and pain points in the experience, i.e., what's going well and what's not
- Understand where channel optimization needs to occur
- Bring in additional customer perspectives and behaviors. (outside of those in the room), shifting the maps from qualitative to more quantitative

- o That is often a requirement to add validity and credibility to the maps
- Shift the perspective from inside out to the outside in in a bigger way (again, shifting from qualitative to quantitative), layering on an additional component of putting the experience in the customer voice
- Make the maps actionable
- Identify—and then prioritize—key moments of truth

Where do you add the data? Well, you've moved your maps to a digital platform, and if you've chosen the right one, you'll be able to add the data into the individual steps of the customer's journey.

In my dream world, digital journey mapping platforms will be integrated with VoC platforms so that the data can flow freely between the two systems, giving brands a much better picture of the customer experience. I know there are journey analytics platforms out there today, but that's not the same thing. My dream is journey analytics on steroids—analytics at such a detailed level that there can be no missteps or bad experiences because you can see, in real-time, where things are broken.

Someday . . .

People will never truly understand something until it happens to them. –Unknown

21 STEP THREE: IDENTIFY

The third step of my journey mapping process is Identify. It's all about identifying and prioritizing moments of truth, researching issues behind them, conducting root cause analysis, developing action plans for updating processes and fixing the customer pain points, assigning owners, doing the work, and measuring outcomes/success.

Before you can know or identify your moments of truth, you must first know what they are. Here's a bit more detail than was offered in Chapter 15.

BusinessDictionary.com defines moment of truth as an *instance of contact or interaction between a customer and a firm (through a product, sales force, or visit) that gives the customer an opportunity to form (or change) an impression about the firm.*

TheFreeDictionary.com states that a moment of truth is *a critical or decisive time on which much depends; a crucial moment.*

Contrary to popular belief, Jan Carlzon didn't come up with the phrase when he wrote his book by the same name. The phrase was first introduced by Richard Normann, who was a strategy consultant for SAS when Carlzon was CEO. Normann defined it as *that moment where quality as perceived by the client is created.*

While Carlzon didn't coin the phrase, he popularized it with his book. Carlzon's definition of "moment of truth" is *anytime a customer comes into contact with any aspect of a business, however remote, is an opportunity to form an impression.* In his book, he states that those moments determine whether the company will succeed or fail and that they are moments when companies must prove to their customers that they are the best alternative.

So you get the idea; it's an important moment. I usually define moment of truth as that make or break moment in the customer journey, that moment when, if all goes well, the customer will continue the journey and complete the task or interaction; he will do (or continue to do) business with you. If things go awry, he will not complete the interaction and will go elsewhere. It's a decision point for the customer.

I don't agree with Carlzon that every touchpoint, every interaction, is a moment of truth. I think he's right that every touchpoint is an opportunity to form an impression, but I don't think every touchpoint becomes a make-or-break point for the customer. Think about the customer journey to purchase a product online, for example. Is every step, every touch critical? No. Every step is certainly important to the process—and perhaps there's a cumulative effect—but there are only a few that will ultimately be make-or-break points for the customer to want to (a) complete that transaction and (b) buy again.

The misconception about journey maps is that they will identify the moments of truth for you. Actually, the maps are only the first step toward identifying them; the data that you incorporate into the maps, as discussed in the previous chapter, are what will identify the moments of truth. This is why it's so critical to include data (VoC, emotions, metrics) in the maps. With data, there's no guesswork as to where or why you're losing customers along the journey.

"Never question the data." That is one of my favorite quotes from Sheen, a character on the Jimmy Neutron series. (That's just between you and me.)

We start this step with using the data to clearly identify the moments of truth. During the journey mapping workshop, customers will guide you to those moments, as well, with their feeling sticky notes and with their votes on the most impactful and either painful or delightful steps along the journey.

Once the moments of truth have been identified, and know that there are multiple moments of truth along the journey, the next step is to prioritize them. Again, the data that you've brought into the map can help you with this. I called this data "business data" in the previous chapter.

But there's a problem. There are a lot of things to fix about the experience. And there are a lot of "competing priorities" in your company. Now what?

You need to help your executives see how all of the improvements go hand in hand with many of the company's other initiatives/priorities—after all, everything you do is for/about the customer, right?! But you also need to, within your own customer experience improvement initiative list, help the executives see some order of priorities.

Yes, they are all important. Customers told you so, right?! And we as customer experience professionals believe it's important to fix everything that breaks the experience. But you know you're not immediately going to get budget to solve all of the world's problems. So as I like to say, let's take some baby steps.

When you go in for the big ask, paint the big picture, i.e., how is it all connected? How do these improvements drive or lead to business outcomes? But also paint the little picture, i.e., help them identify, within your list of immediate needs, which are more immediate than others.

There are a lot of different ways to prioritize your customer experience improvement initiatives. You determine the ways that speak most loudly to your executives. They may include looking at:

- Cost to fix
- Time to fix

- Effort to fix
- Resources required to fix
- Portion of customers it affects
- Which customer (persona) it affects
- Impact on the customer
- Impact on the business

Know that they are not linear; the prioritization typically requires a combination of two or more of these metrics. I recommend that that combination always includes "impact on the customer," i.e., what is most important to the customer? What matters most to the customer? If we do this and not that, will the customer stay or leave?

Why? Because it's all about the customer! Everything you do as a business.

If you always frame the prioritization that way, it should also speak volumes to your executives, especially when you tell them that if certain actions aren't taken, you will lose X percent of customers. In order to get executive commitment, you need to build the business case. This holds true for prioritizing the improvement initiatives as well. Build the business case, tie it to business outcomes, and speak their language.

Another approach to consider when thinking about impact on the business and impact on the customer: two models that come out of *Harvard Business Review,* the Apostle Model and the Loyalty-Profitability Model.

The Apostle Model segments customers by combining their loyalty with their satisfaction levels, allowing you to identify and then to place greater priority on those things that will help you keep your most loyal and most satisfied customers.

On the other hand, the Loyalty-Profitability Model segments customers by combining their loyalty with their profitability, allowing you to identify and to place greater priority on what it takes to keep your most valuable customers.

Both of them provide roundabout ways to prioritize initiatives by prioritizing customers. These models also help you understand why taking a two-dimensional (or more) approach to prioritization paints a better picture.

One other option is to conduct a So What exercise, which allows you to identify the importance and the impact of implementing an improvement solution. This methodology was developed by the US Army to move beyond simply uncovering root causes to prioritizing—and then actually implementing—ideal, impactful improvements. It allows you to identify the impact of various improvement initiatives and weigh them against each other, getting at the list of top initiatives that best support desired company and customer outcomes.

Having said all that, ultimately, this prioritization has to be based on criteria that were established by the governance structure, namely, the executive steering committee. The committee will take a look at all of the company's initiatives and prioritize one relative to another; when they do this, I would simply ask that they remember: you are in business for and because of the customer. Put the customer first. "Competing priorities" are a myth.

I've already written about root cause analysis and action planning in Chapter 11. Revisit that chapter to identify next steps. But Step Three rounds out with:

- Conducting root cause analysis
- Developing action plans for updating processes and fixing pain points
- Taking the plans to the executive committee to add to initiatives roadmap and review/approve alongside other initiatives
- Getting approval for budget and resources
- Assigning owners and deadlines
- Having them build out project plans
- Fixing the pain points
- Measuring outcomes/success

This step is really all about making immediate, incremental improvements to the experience—until we can get through Step Five, in which we'll ideate and redesign the entire experience (or portions of it that need to be overhauled).

But first, on to Step Four . . .

Things which matter most must never be at the mercy of things which matter least. –Johann Wolfgang von Goethe

22 STEP FOUR: INTROSPECT

I have dubbed this step "the secret sauce to achieve outcomes with journey mapping." It's such a critical step, and quite honestly, I think most people aren't even aware of this step. That, my friends, is a big reason for journey mapping fails.

Why? Because you can't fix what's happening on the outside (for the customer) if you don't fix what's happening on the inside to support and facilitate the experience.

What am I referring to? Service blueprinting.

A service blueprint looks inward and outlines the people, policies, tools, and systems that support and facilitate the customer experience; it visualizes the relationship between different service components that are directly tied to the steps in the journey you just mapped. And it helps you hone in on the root causes of customer pain points.

It also includes a process map, which outlines the workflows that do the same, to correspond with the customer journey you've mapped. You can include the processes in the service blueprint or do a separate and corresponding process map; I prefer including it.

The service blueprint drills into the steps, processes, and hand-offs that work "backstage" to ensure the delivery of a consistent, efficient, and intentional customer experience. It is used to identify root causes of customer experience pain points, to improve an existing experience, or to design a new experience.

By linking the service blueprint to the customer's journey, you've got that end-to-end picture of the journey plus the customer-to-core view of the organizational support and delivery of the experience, giving you the complete picture of what's working and what's not. Without this complete view, you cannot make meaningful systemic changes to how you serve the customer and to their experience. This view is critical to your root cause analysis.

The image below depicts the typical swim lanes of a service blueprint, with descriptions following, after the picture.

Service Blueprint Template – Current State

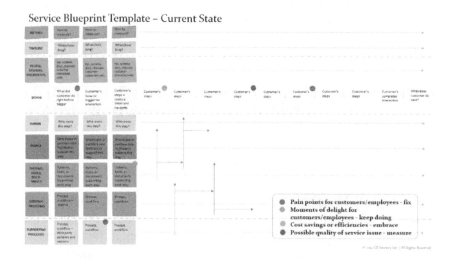

Onstage Details

These are the only two components that you bring over from—or use to link to—the journey map.

Yellow sticky notes: what the customer is doing. These are the steps that the customer took to complete whatever experience it was that you/they mapped.

Bright blue sticky notes: the people, systems, documents, and other physical items, e.g., signs, insurance card, phone, app, that the customer used, touched, or interacted with along their journey.

Backstage Details

Backstage refers to the people, tools, systems, processes, policies, and more that correspond to delivering the journey that was mapped.

Gray sticky notes: the owner of the step. I wrote in Chapter 21 about the importance of assigning step owners upon completion of the map.

Dark blue sticky notes: the people (employees or partners) who facilitate or support this step.

Bright pink sticky notes: the systems, tools, policies, or documents that facilitate or support this step.

Purple sticky notes: the process or workflow that enables each step—and then all steps collectively.

Behind-the-Scene Details

We differentiate backstage from behind-the-scenes so that we can attribute the processes accordingly and get to the source for correction.

Gold sticky notes: the supporting processes, as provided by external partners or vendors.

Time and Metrics

These are two pieces of information that may also be pulled over with the journey map.

Light blue sticky notes: time it took for each step; a timeline of the journey.

Green sticky notes: any data or metrics that will help to tell the story of the experience, e.g., hold time, wait time, number of clicks, and other operational data, as noted in Chapter 20.

Dotted Lines

You'll notice that there are multiple dotted horizontal lines through the service blueprint.

The first one separates time and metrics from the next section, which houses the customer actions and touchpoints (people, systems, documents, etc.).

The next line is referred to as the line of visibility, which separates what the customer sees on stage from what the customer doesn't see backstage. The customer cannot see into the business or cannot see what's happening behind this line.

And the last line at the bottom of the image is the line of internal interaction, which puts a break between backstage and behind-the-scenes, the point where the organization interacts with external vendors and partners to deliver the experience. The customer has no visibility into this.

Lines and Arrows

You'll also notice that there are lines and arrows once you get below the line of visibility. These lines and arrows show the flow and direction of the interactions happening to deliver the service, the exchange of value occurring, and who/what controls the exchange or action at that step in the journey.

Dots

And finally, there are some colorful dots on the blueprint, which work similar to the dots on the journey map, but not quite. These dots are rooted in customer and employee feedback about what's working and what's not.

They allow us to identify the backstage components that are (or contribute to)...

- Root causes for pain points that the customer experienced
- Inefficiencies in the service delivery process
- Service components that must be fixed or improved
- Opportunities to measure the quality of the service
- Opportunities for cost savings or increased profits
- Moments that are loved by the customer and should not be lost

Specifically, the red and green dots can be pulled from the journey map to highlight service areas that are pain points or high points for customers, especially those that are moments of truth. The blue and purple dots will come from internal feedback, from employees and stakeholders who feel the pain or understand the root causes of customer pain. The blue dots call out areas for cost savings or other efficiencies, while the purple dots highlight root causes of issues that need to be evaluated. You can, of course, add more dots/other colors to bring in more details—whatever helps you identify what's working and what's broken, how to prioritize (cost, resources, etc. data), and more.

As you go through this process of building out your service blueprint, you will uncover something quite scary, something that is totally counter to what this book is about, i.e., putting the "customer" in *customer* experience. You will uncover that your internal systems, tools, policies, and processes were not designed with the customer in mind, at all.

It's time to change that. Service blueprints are important to understanding the current experience, understanding who and what are involved in delivering the current experience, improving the existing experience, and designing a new experience.

As you've read this chapter, I think you've probably gotten a better sense for why this is the secret sauce in the journey mapping process. If you only focus on fixing the issues you see on the outside (onstage), the things the customer tells you are broken, then you're likely only applying lipstick to a pig, making cosmetic changes. But if you take the time to dig deep, to understand the inner workings and how they all flow and interact in order to deliver the experience, you'll have a better picture of what needs to be done differently. And you'll have the tools and the knowledge to make the changes that will significantly impact and improve the experience the customer is having.

Hold that thought. It's time to go design an entirely new experience.

Without the intentional design of backstage systems and operations, the work of navigating them is outsourced to the customer. –Kendra L. Schimmel, Capital One

ENDNOTES

There are various sources that I have researched over the years to guide me on this process. I'm certainly not excluding them from my endnotes intentionally. Happy to source or provide sources, should you request/require them.

23 STEP FIVE: IDEATE

You've made it this far. Don't give up yet. It's time for some fun. Yes, journey mapping is/can be fun! I've called this step Ideate because it involves ideating, and then mapping, the ideal experience for your customers with your customers.

One important thing to note, which I've mentioned previously, is this: don't think you can start your journey mapping process here. You've got to map out the current state before you can design the future state, as I've already outlined in my six-step process. You can't transform something you don't understand. You don't want to change things that are working well or that create value for your customers. So know the current state and what to fix and what to maintain before designing the future state.

Future-state journey mapping serves many purposes, including:

- Identifying and examining future experiences or journeys in collaboration with real customers
- Co-creating and designing the ideal experience with customers
- Co-creating and designing a differentiated experience with customers
- Envisioning what the experience could look like in the future at minimal risk because it's tested first on paper

Okay, where to begin?

While current-state and future-state workshops are for very different purposes and have different outcomes, some parts of the process are similar. (More on the future-state mapping process in a minute.) The linkage between the two maps themselves is that the future-state maps are rooted in the outputs or learnings from the current-state maps. This means that you'll choose which experiences to redesign based on what customers identified as painful experiences during current-state mapping. Yes, you will have made some tactical improvements to the experience since then, but ultimately, customers will expect you to overhaul and simplify the experience.

During the planning stage for the future-state mapping workshop, you'll define objectives and outcomes, outline the scope of the map (based on problems you identified and need to solve as a result of the current-state map), identify the personas for which you'll design the new experience, recruit customers and stakeholders to participate in the workshop, and conduct pre-workshop sessions with each to discuss guidelines, goals, and what they need to think about or bring (if anything).

One of the things that you'll need to consider as you plan out the future-state mapping workshop is the ideation approach that you'll use. One of the fun things you'll do during this workshop is ideation, which is a creative process to generate new ideas. It is focused on the quantity of ideas you come up with over quality.

And, no, I'm not just using a fancy word for brainstorming; brainstorming is a form of ideation. There are many different ideation approaches, so it's important beforehand to identify the ideation approach you're going to use. Interaction Design Institute offers up a variety of options: https://www.interaction-design.org/literature/topics/ideation.

I'll go into more details about your ideation and future-state mapping workshop in Chapter 31.

It's also time to develop the future-state service blueprint. The one big difference between this and future-state mapping is the audience: future-state journey maps are created with customers, while future-state service blueprinting is done with stakeholders and employee subject matter experts—after the future-state mapping workshop.

***

A quick sidebar on the reasons for involving the employee subject matter experts for the specific experience in the service blueprint workshops.

The first reason is the obvious one: they know the systems, tools, processes, and policies involved in delivering that experience better than anyone.

The second reason is this basic change principle: involve employees, and they will adopt and adapt. There's a great quote from Benjamin Franklin that's so fitting here: *"Tell me and I forget. Teach me and I may remember. Involve me and I learn."*

Get employees involved—early in the process. When that happens, they feel like they're a part of it. Don't just force change on them; give them a voice and some ownership in the change. They'll be more accepting of it, without a doubt.

***

Back to future-state service blueprinting. It allows you to:

- Conduct root cause analyses for pain points customer experienced
- Identify inefficiencies in the service delivery process
- Ideate solutions and capabilities to deliver the future-state experience you've mapped and designed with customers.
- Design the service delivery capabilities of the future-state experience.
- Test on paper how the future-state service delivery will play out before implementing.

During the planning stage for the future-state service blueprint workshop, you'll define objectives and outcomes; outline the scope of the blueprint (based on future-state design you want to implement); do some of the pre-work for the blueprint, such as linking it to the customer journey and bringing in steps and data from the future-state customer journey map; identify the stakeholders and employee subject matter experts to participate in the workshop; and identify the ideation approach you'll use during the workshop.

I'll go into more detail when I take you through the workshops in the next section of the book, starting with Chapter 25.

The secret of change is to focus all of your energy, not on fighting the old, but on building the new. –Socrates

24 STEP SIX: IMPLEMENT

The last step in the journey mapping process is the one that will make all the difference! It's time to get to work. It's time to take everything you've learned in the Ideate step—actually, throughout this whole process—and put it to work.

Unfortunately, this is where things often fall apart—if they haven't fallen apart long before this. You've followed the process. You've done things right. You've got all of this great information. Please go do something with it. Please execute and implement!

Where do you begin? Well, the future-state journey map and the future-state service blueprint become the blueprints or statement of direction for the work to be done. Use them to guide you to develop the new experience.

You've designed the experience; now you've got to prototype it, test it with a subset of customers, and fail fast—lather, rinse, and repeat—until customers love it. You can't afford to get it wrong at this point; make sure the new experience matches what you heard from customers during this journey mapping process.

Once you've pilot tested with a small group of customers and gotten their approval, you've got to roll out the experience to all customers. When you do that, you must remember to do the following, which may seem like no-brainers, but trust me, I wouldn't write about them if they truly were.

Train Employees

If you want employees to deliver a new experience, they've got to be trained on the new systems, tools, policies, and processes put in place to deliver the experience. And they've also got to be trained on how to actually deliver the new experience. What are customers' expectations? How do employees ensure they are meeting those expectations and providing the best experience for their customers? You can use the journey maps and service blueprints for this training.

Close the Loop with Customers

The experience has changed; don't surprise customers. You've got to let them know that the experience has changed and why. You've also got to let them know about new tools, systems, processes, and people they'll be interacting with to do whatever it is that they'll be trying to do during this experience.

Update the Maps

Your journey maps should always reflect the most current state of the customer experience. This means that the future-state map becomes the current-state map—with a few tweaks and some input from customers.

One of the most popular questions I'm asked when I speak about journey mapping is, "*When should I update the maps?*" Or "*How frequently should I update the maps?*" There are several scenarios that are catalysts for updating the map:

- Any time the experience is improved, the maps should be updated to reflect the new current state.
- If you get feedback that the experience has new pain points or that it no longer meets customers' evolving needs, then you need to map again and identify where things are breaking down and how design a better experience.
- If the product has changed, how the product is delivered has changed, or if you are offering new products and

services, you'll want to map again.

- If your company has merged with or acquired another business, you should map or re-map because a lot of things will have changed – for both employees and customers.

Ultimately, when to update your maps really depends on your customers, your business, your industry; as each of these evolves, so will the experience. But the number-one deciding factor for when it's time to map again is whether the experience has changed, e.g., improvements were made, feedback was received that something is broken.

Action is the foundational key to all success. –Pablo Picasso

Annette Franz

WORKSHOPS

Annette Franz

25 WORKSHOP GUIDELINES

This may just be the section of the book for which you bought the book. Thank you for reading this far! I'm sure you realize that the background and the process are important to know and to understand.

This first chapter on workshops will cover rules of engagement, participant responsibilities, sample agendas, workshop supplies, and more. I'll get into the meat of the current-state mapping workshop in the next chapter.

Workshop Supplies

Let's start with supplies. Since I like to start journey mapping with butcher paper and sticky notes—and then digitize the map—this is what I've got in my supplies bag.

- *Butcher paper*: it comes in huge rolls, so bring about 20 feet per map, to be safe. I like to take two sheets per map, one to map on and one to cover the map with before rolling it up. That's my preference, and you may not find that second sheet necessary.
- *3" x 3" sticky notes in a variety of colors*: I'll make color recommendations as I go through the workshop in an upcoming chapter, but you can use whatever colors you'd like to use.
- *4" x 6" sticky notes*: to label the swim lanes of the map.

- *Black fine-point markers*: participants will use these to write on the sticky notes.
- *Clear packing tape*: you'll need this to tape down all of the sticky notes onto the butcher paper when you're done mapping. If you don't tape them down, be prepared to unravel and pick up a mess of loose sticky notes.
- *Scotch tape*: just in case you need it.
- *Scissors*: to cut butcher paper, tape, etc.
- *Rubber bands*: to put around the map after it's rolled up.
- *Flip charts or large-sheet sticky notes*: use these for the parking lot items, i.e., other journeys to map, big ideas, etc.
- *Red and green dots*: these are the stickers you'll use for voting/emotions. I found some fun red and green stickers with smiley and frowny faces on them on Amazon.
- *Blue and purple dots*: you'll need these for the service blueprint workshop. You might as well pick up a variety of colors, as you may have need for additional colors of dots.
- *Nametags/labels*: for attendees.
- *Snacks/beverages*: these aren't in my supplies bag, but you need to bring them to every workshop to keep energy levels up!

Rules of Engagement

When you get into the workshop, you've got to set some ground rules and rules of engagement. You've got to make sure your stakeholders are engaged—in the right way, at the right time. Some of these seem like no brainers, but you'll find that you have to remind participants.

1. Listen.

Pay attention. Let your customers talk and do the talking. Listen to what they tell you about the experience. Hear what they say.

2. Focus on People (Customers)

This sounds like a no-brainer, but focusing on customers is a fundamental part of design thinking and human-centered design. If you want to innovate successfully, you must continually focus on meeting customer needs. So you need to focus first on the people in this exercise. It's all about them. It's all about their story.

3. Empathize

Empathy is a fundamental attitude that informs the discipline of design. This is one area where journey mapping becomes a strong tool in the design thinking toolbox. It places a priority on understanding emotion. This is sometimes a warm and fuzzy kind of thing that people roll their eyes at. But it can be as simple as asking yourself: What was she feeling when that happened? How did that step make her feel?

Let me tell you, even the toughest, least touchy-feely industries appreciate this part of the process. It's an eye-opener.

4. Be Curious

As you listen and observe, continually question what is going on and why. What just happened? Why did she do that? How did he decide what to do next? Ask questions. No questions are stupid. But ask them at the appropriate time during the workshop.

5. Have an Open Mind

Let go of what you think you know about your customers and about the experience. Let go of any preconceived notions about what happened, why it happened, or what is possible. Let your walls down. Be open to what others are saying about the experience. About challenges. About potential solutions. You'll be amazed!

Participant Responsibilities

In order to have a successful workshop, all participants must know and understand their roles and responsibilities. They should have all been prepped in advance during their pre-workshop prep meetings, but it's never a bad thing to remind them all again, once they get into the room. Here's what you need them to do.

Customers

The most important things for customers to do is to participate! That seems simple enough, but we need all customer participants to get up out of their seats, engaged, working together, talking to each other, questioning, and putting a solid piece of work up on the wall for you and your stakeholders to understand the experience.

They also need to share the artifacts that they brought; they need to think about the appropriate place to add them to the map.

It's worth repeating that they should be asking each other questions and questioning everything. What about that? Did this happen to you? Did you need to do that next? What came next? Then what happened?

They will probably designate someone as the writer, the main person putting sticky notes up on the butcher paper, but they may also decide to just add their own sticky notes as something comes up. Either way, they'll need to self-regulate and self-coordinate to ensure that they put a cohesive product up on the wall.

They will then also need to designate someone to do the readout to the stakeholders once the map is done.

Stakeholders

I've already addressed a lot of this in the Rules of Engagement section, but the main thing that stakeholders need to do while customers are mapping is to listen. Listen and observe. Don't judge what's being said, and don't be defensive. They'll get to ask questions later but shouldn't be afraid to answer customer questions if/as they arise. You, as the facilitator, will answer most of the questions, but occasionally, a stakeholder may be better suited to respond.

Workshop Agenda

The agenda for the workshop will vary depending on a few factors, including how many maps you'll be creating, the complexity of the maps, whether you'll be current-state and future-state mapping in the same workshops, and for how many different personas. I've done full-day workshops, and I've done half-day workshops. I think it's safe to say that most people prefer the half-day workshop, but sometimes, you have to adjust and adapt!

The agenda for a typical half-day workshop in which you're mapping one experience with two different personas, i.e., two different maps, looks like this. You'll note that the first hour is set up and then housekeeping items. The workshop itself begins at 8:30

and runs through 1:30, with a break in the middle.

Time	Topic	Owner
8:00-8:30	Workshop setup, arrivals	Facilitator
8:30-8:45	Introductions, agenda, ground rules	Facilitator
8:45-9:00	Scope/journeys personas explained	Facilitator
9:00-11:00	Journey mapping	Customers
11:00-11:15	Break	
11:15-12:15	Map #1 readout and Q&A	Persona #1
12:15-1:15	Map #2 readout and Q&A	Persona #2
1:15-1:30	Wrap-up and next steps	Facilitator

A full-day workshop, in which perhaps you're doing one future-state map in the second half of the day, looks like this. You could also adjust or adapt this to create additional current-state maps in the second half of the day, e.g., same two personas, different journeys or two new personas, same journey.

Time	Topic	Owner
8:00-8:30	Workshop setup, arrivals	Facilitator
8:30-8:45	Introductions, agenda, ground rules	Facilitator
8:45-9:00	Scope/journeys personas explained	Facilitator
9:00-11:00	Journey mapping	Customers
11:00-11:15	Break	
11:15-12:00	Map #1 readout and Q&A	Persona #1
12:00-12:45	Map #2 readout and Q&A	Persona #2
12:45-1:30	Lunch	
1:30-1:45	Explain ideation and future-state mapping	Facilitator
1:45-2:45	Ideation session	Facilitator
2:45-4:45	Future-state mapping	Customers
4:45-5:30	Map #1 readout and Q&A	Persona #1
5:30-6:15	Map #2 readout and Q&A	Persona #2

That's a long day. (I'd recommend a cocktail reception for everyone after that!)

Don't short-change the future-state mapping exercise if you're doing it in the second half of the day. It's extremely important. I'd recommend that you shift future-state mapping to a second workshop day, just to be safe. But I've provided the sample workshop because I've been asked about this type of agenda.

The agenda examples are only rough or loose guidelines. The actual times will fluctuate and vary, depending on when you start, the journeys you map, the problems to be solved, and more. There's also no time built in for a break in the afternoon session, so adjust for that or bring in snacks and drinks to keep everyone nourished and hydrated—and know that people will step out here and there to use the restroom.

Let's move on to workshop setup. I'm going to assume that: you've secured a room, recruited customers and stakeholders, had your pre-workshop prep meetings, told customers and stakeholders date, time, and location, and are ready to conduct the workshop.

It's not only moving that creates new starting points. Sometimes all it takes is a subtle shift in perspective, an opening of the mind, an intentional pause and reset, or a new route to start to see new options and new possibilities. –Kristin Armstrong

26 WORKSHOP SETUP AND HOUSEKEEPING

Let's work our way through the flow of a workshop, starting with setup and housekeeping items before the actual mapping begins.

Workshop Setup

Encourage customers and stakeholders to arrive about ten to fifteen minutes before the workshop start time (you know there will be stragglers) so that you can begin on time. You should arrive at the workshop site at least thirty to forty-five minutes before the workshop begins so that you can set up the room. It matters less how the chairs/tables are set up and more about having wall space and room for people to stand around that wall space to talk and map.

If you cut the butcher paper before you arrive at the workshop location, you'll simply need to tape it to the wall. Be sure the wall surface can handle tape, e.g., if you're in a hotel conference room covered with wallpaper, that's a non-starter; you can't tape anything to those walls. For flat, painted, non-wallpapered walls, it will be easier to get this paper on the wall if you've got a partner who can hold/tape one end while you tape the other.

Next, you'll take the 4" x 6" sticky notes and label the swim lanes. You'll need swim lanes for: Timeline; Channel; Systems, Tools, Documents; People; Environmental Factors; Feeling;

Thinking; and Doing. Place them in that order on the butcher paper, from top to bottom. The bottom/first swim lane (that customers will see in the workshop) should be what the customer is Doing. The first column in the image below is an example of how to label each swim lane.

Journey Map Template – Current State

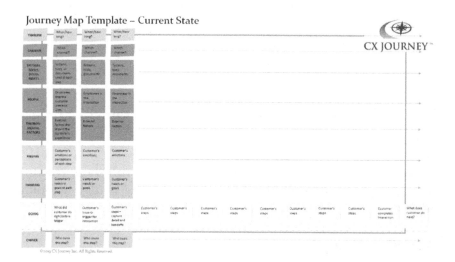

Next, you'll want to make sure all of the sticky notes are out on a table and organized in a way that you know which one you'll hand to customers as you introduce the next swim lane for them to work on. Have the black markers close by as well.

By now, people should be arriving. Ask them to check-in, fill out a nametag/label and wear it, and have a seat. Be sure to have drinks and snacks for everyone to grab before getting started too.

Start the workshop by making introductions, reviewing the agenda, talking about why everyone is here, and covering the ground rules.

Ground Rules

As you begin the workshop, you should lay out ground rules for the workshop in order to get everyone in the right mindset and to ensure they stay on task. You can add your own, of course, but here are some things to get you started.

- No cell phones or laptops—customers or stakeholders.
- Customers: You are the customer; put on your customer hat and walk through the steps you have taken as you've gone on this journey to do X. We want to understand what your experience was as if we were there with you.
- Use "I statements" and try to write out complete thoughts on the sticky notes so that we understand what was happening or what you were thinking or feeling.
- Think "details;" don't skip any steps, including things you think are outside of our control or things that happen between steps, e.g., waiting, driving, etc.
- Keep an open mind; question everything.
- Don't problem solve; capture solutions and "big ideas" on the "parking lot" on the wall.
- If you come to a fork in the road, capture it and move on. Stick to the defined scope of the map.
- Capture those micro-journeys or other journeys to be mapped on the "parking lot."
- If you have questions about what you're doing, please ask.
- Ask each other questions: What's happened next? What else? Participate.

Talk about the scope of the journeys to be mapped and the personas for which you're mapping. Start with personas; tell the story of who they are, their pain points and problems, and their desired outcomes for the journey to be mapped. Spend a little time on the scope: what you're mapping, the start and endpoint, what happened right before and right after, what got you there? You'll likely work with each group to lay the first sticky note with them.

Answer any questions that attendees may have, split them up into two groups according to their personas, and then instruct them to get up out of their chairs; it's time to journey map!

Have a bias toward action. Let's see something happen now. You can break that big plan into small steps and take the first step right away. –Indira Gandhi

Annette Franz

27 CURRENT-STATE MAPPING WORKSHOP

Customers should have markers in hand and be equipped with the first color of sticky notes that they're going to use. I'll give my color recommendations in this chapter, but you can change them accordingly; while shopping, you might not find the colors I mention. Just be sure each swim lane is a different color.

Let's get started!

What is the Customer Doing?
Grab the PALE YELLOW sticky notes. The first thing that customers are going to put up on the butcher paper is what they were doing—the steps that they took to start the journey until they achieved what they were trying to do. Start (or go back and add) one sticky note that states what they were doing or what happened right before this journey began. Perhaps it outlines what caused them to go on this journey. Have them provide detailed steps; don't skip anything, e.g., parking, driving, transfers, call escalations, etc.

How Long Did That Take?
Next, grab the PALE BLUE sticky notes and have the participants put up a timeline that corresponds with the steps that they just put on the wall. You've already labeled the swim lanes, so they should just follow your labeling scheme to find where to place these sticky notes. They should place a sticky note to correspond

with the Doing sticky notes. What we want to see is how much time each step took and how long it took to go from start to finish.

OnStage Experience

Next, we want to know who and what customers interacted with in order to complete the task. Have them use the BRIGHT PINK sticky notes to jot down the people they interacted with at each step of the journey, and then use the BRIGHT BLUE sticky notes to capture the systems, tools, or documents they used. Examples of these include website, app, invoice, receipt, forms, signage, insurance card, checkout line, credit card terminal, etc.

Channels

In some regards, channels may be redundant with the bright blue sticky notes used above, but not in every case. Use the BROWN sticky note to capture through which channel they interacted at each step of the journey. Examples include: phone, website, mail, in-store, social media, video chat, chat, text message, etc.

Artifacts

This is a good time to collect the artifacts that customers brought to share about this journey. Ask if anyone brought artifacts. If they did, collect the artifacts, label/number them each A1, A2, A3, etc. and then have them place an "A#" on the BRIGHT BLUE sticky note that corresponds with the artifact. You can then go back and put the two pieces together when you're back in the office. Ultimately, you'll scan the artifacts and import them into your digitized map.

What is the Customer Thinking?

Have customers grab the ORANGE sticky note and document their specific needs and goals at the moment, at each step. What were they trying to achieve in that step? Note that not every step/pale yellow sticky note will have a corresponding orange sticky note/goal.

What is the Customer Feeling?

Capturing customer emotions is one of the most important things that we can learn and understand as part of this process. It's when customers tell you that they were frustrated or felt like you didn't care about them that you begin to humanize the experience, unfortunately. But it's true. And it's real. So give customers the PEACH sticky note and have them document their feelings and emotions along each step of the journey. As with Thinking, customers may not have a Feeling for every step in the journey, and that's okay.

What Environmental Factors Impact the Experience?
This step isn't always captured in journey mapping workshops, but environmental factors that impact the experience are important to identify and know. These are things that are outside of your control but that you've got to mitigate, design for, or design around. They could affect your ability to improve the experience or to innovate. Don't let these factors be the reason that you're losing customers!

Ask customers to grab the GREEN sticky note and place the letters P, S, T, E, L, or Ec on the sticky note with a brief explanation, like this:

Here's what the letters stand for:

- Political
- Social
- Technological
- Environmental
- Legal
- Economic

The Map is Almost Done
That's it for sticky notes! Your map should look pretty full and detailed right now. If it's looking sparse, ask customers if they've

thought of everything or if they need help with a particular section of the journey.

Throughout all of that work, stakeholders are simply listening and observing. You, as the facilitator, are splitting your time between the two groups of customers who are mapping, answering questions and coaching them along as they build out their maps.

Next up, you'll be asking customers to evaluate their attitudes on the map.

Evaluate Attitudes

In this step, you'll give each customer three red dot stickers and three green dot stickers. They'll use the red dot stickers to vote for the steps along the journey that caused them the most pain or where their goals were not met, and they'll use the green dots to vote for the steps where your company delighted them, and their goals were met. They can place all dots of a color on one step or spread them out across three different steps.

When you see clusters of red dots or green dots on a particular step, these are potential moments of truth. You'll validate and verify that later, when you add data and metrics into the map. For now, the red dot clusters are pain points in the experience, while the green dot clusters are the high points, things that you want to keep doing well.

At this point, your customers are finished mapping. You might ask them to take a quick look to make sure they can't add anything else. If not, then it's storytelling time!

Readout: Experience Explained

Now that the map is done, we want to hear the story from customers' mouths. We want them to tell the story of their experience: their steps, their goals along the way, and the feelings elicited by the experience. Ask them to delegate one person to take you through the story of the experience. Have the designated person start from the beginning, including what happened right before and the catalyst for this experience. As they walk through the steps, have them explain: Why did you do that? What was the reason or the goal behind that step? Why did you feel that way? Who else was involved? How did the onstage people and systems impact the experience or contribute to the moment?

Up to this point, they may not have realized yet that they put the whole story of their experience up on the wall; as they talk through it, they certainly will! And you and your colleagues want to hear the story in their words. This is a powerful portion of the mapping workshop as stakeholders start to feel the full effect of the current experience on their customers.

This is the point where stakeholders not only listen but can also ask questions for clarification and more details. They shouldn't be defensive; instead, they should listen, ask, and respond to learn and to understand.

Upon completion of the readout and Q&A, thank everyone for their time and participation. In B2C scenarios, be sure to follow up with customers regarding their incentives. For B2B workshops, you might move from the workshop to that cocktail reception or happy hour that I mentioned earlier.

We learn from hearing about it, seeing it done, then doing it ourselves. –Nina Allen Freeman

28 AFTER THE WORKSHOP

This chapter is probably the most important one in the book! I wanted this to be its own chapter so that this next step doesn't get buried in the workshop chapter. It's an important step on its own.

You've mapped, but now, it's time to figure out next steps. Keep the momentum going—don't just return to the office and shove the maps under your desk. You've got your work cut out for you. Remember, the maps are just the beginning; they are a catalyst for change, but they can't be that when they're stashed in a safe place.

So what's next?

The day after the workshop, host a debrief meeting with your stakeholder participants. Hang the maps on the wall for all to see again. Ask for their feedback, insights, and interpretations of what they heard and learned.

Next, have them assign owners (people, not departments) to each of the steps in the journey, paying careful attention to those steps that garnered the most red dots and the most green dots. Why do you need owners? When we assign owners to each step of the journey, we:

- Know who is responsible for fixing what's broken
- Know who to commend for what's going well

- Increase actionability of the map
- Empower change, where needed
- Identify lack of ownership (which could be a problem or the root cause of a problem)
- See how different departments interact and are involved to deliver the experience
- Open the doors to break down and/or connect silos

Beyond that, discuss and identify next steps and develop a closed-loop process, i.e., what's this improvement process going to look like from today through when improvements to the experience are made and then communicated to employees and customers? Do not leave that meeting without a plan for moving forward. Most importantly, make sure you incorporate Step Three: Identify into your next steps. Go back to Chapter 21 if you need a refresher on what that step entails.

If you're a B2B company and have just mapped 1:1 with accounts (rather than a workshop with multiple customers/accounts in the room), conduct a debrief call with the customer a day or two after the workshop for additional feedback or thoughts post-workshop. They've had some time to think about what was discussed during the workshop and may have some other perspectives and feedback to share with you.

Be sure to digitize the maps. You've got to get them out of paper format and into a format that ensures they become a living, breathing document. (Take the butcher paper map and hang it in your customer room to share with employees.) Next, add data and metrics to the map and give access to those who are working on initiatives arising out of this map.

You'll also need to prepare a report of findings, insights (e.g., gaps in the experience, in listening posts, etc.), and recommendations based on what you've heard and learned. Schedule a readout of the findings and recommendations to stakeholders and anyone else they deem relevant, governance committees, and step owners assigned to the steps in the map.

Speaking of which, you'll need to keep the governance committees informed of the findings and keep committee members in the loop as action planning and then the work progresses. You'll need to share your findings and action plans with the executive committee to get prioritization and budget/resource approval; they'll weigh your improvement projects with other initiatives on the master roadmap. Your job will be to build the case and ensure initiatives coming out of this mapping work become a priority relative to everything else.

If you're a B2B company and have mapped 1:1 with an account, once you've determined your action plan and have received approval to move forward, schedule a call with the account to review your plan and next steps. Get additional insights from them, as needed or as offered. Keep the customer in the loop to ensure that the issue(s) get resolved to their satisfaction. Remember that I mentioned that this 1:1 mapping approach can be a relationship builder? Don't blow it. Fix the problem and communicate the solution.

In case you aren't keeping track, next up is Step Four: Introspect. I've already written about that in Chapter 22, so I'll outline the service blueprint workshop that you'll prepare for and conduct next.

Never confuse movement for action. – Ernest Hemingway

Annette Franz

29 SERVICE BLUEPRINT WORKSHOP

Remember—if you want to fix what's happening on the outside, you've got to fix what's happening inside. Let's walk through a service blueprint workshop. I've covered a lot of this in Chapter 22, Step Four: Introspect, but this chapter includes a few more details.

What is the Scope of the Blueprint?

The scope is defined by the outcomes/output of the journey map. In other words, once you've identified painful steps and, especially, moments of truth in the current-state experience, you'll need to take a look beneath the covers to identify the root cause and outline how you'll improve that. The service blueprint will be a key step to resolving any future issues with the experience for the customer.

Is the scope impacted by personas? To some degree, yes, but less so than the actual journey map. There will still be twists and turns and differences in the journey as it varies by persona, so those should be accounted for in the service blueprint. It may be easier to capture all of those twists and turns in one service blueprint because that may highlight where and why other parts of the journey—and for other personas—the experience breaks down.

Who Participates?

Service blueprint workshops are 100 percent internal. These workshops are about your internal people and processes that support and facilitate the experience the customer is having.

So who should you invite to participate? Start with the scope of the map. Once you know the scope, you know who to invite: the stakeholders, key stakeholders, subject matter experts for this journey, and owners assigned to the steps of the customer's journey after the journey mapping workshop.

Having all these folks in the room helps to align stakeholders and break down or connect silos as well. When everyone understands the desired outcome and the purpose of this work (the customer, the customer experience), it helps to get people marching in the same/right direction.

Where Do You Begin?
First things first—get your workshop space set up; it will be very similar to what you did for the current-state workshop. Put your butcher paper on the wall, lay out your tools, and set up the room in a way that's conducive for participation and discussion. You should have the current-state journey map for which you're creating the service blueprint hung in the room.

Next, on your butcher paper, lay out the steps of the customer journey for which you're developing the service blueprint. In other words, bring over the sticky notes from the current-state map swim lane labeled "Doing." (Figuratively. Don't actually pull them off the current-state map; copy the same steps from that map onto the blueprint.)

Then, add the timing and onstage components from the current-state map to the service blueprint butcher paper. These swim lanes were labeled, "Timeline," "People," and "Systems, Tools, Documents" on your current-state map. You've got step owners in the room, so I would also add the "Step Owner" from the current-state map into the foundation for the service blueprint. The colors for the sticky notes are outlined in Chapter 22, but to remind you:

- Customer Doing: YELLOW
- Timeline: LIGHT BLUE

- Onstage People: BRIGHT BLUE
- Onstage Systems, Tools, Documents: BRIGHT PINK
- Step Owner: GRAY

Getting Started

Now that you've got all of the onstage items identified for the experience you're delivering on, and you've got your participants in the room, explain to them what it is that you're looking to accomplish in the day's workshop, i.e., the experience you're improving, the current state, and any details they need in order to have perspective for what this workshop is all about.

The Backstage People

To get started with the blueprint, give your participants DARK BLUE sticky notes to identify the people, either employees or partners, who facilitate and support each step of the journey up on the wall.

The Backstage Systems, Tools, Policies

Next up, participants need to add the systems, tools, and policies that support or facilitate each step of the customer journey. Use BRIGHT PINK sticky notes to add these.

Backstage Processes

After stakeholders have mapped the systems, tools, and policies, you need to capture processes or internal workflow that facilitate each step. Use PURPLE sticky notes to capture this workflow, but don't be afraid to use arrows to help with this as well.

Behind-the-Scene Details

We differentiate backstage from behind-the-scenes so that we can attribute the processes accordingly and get to the source for correction. Behind-the-scenes processes refer to those tools, systems, and processes provided by third-party vendors. Give your participants GOLD sticky notes to identify supporting processes provided by external partners and vendors. (This is a good reminder to next map your vendor experience and processes!)

Timeline and Metrics

You've already added the timeline from the customer's perspective while you were setting up the workshop, so next up, add some data or metrics that will help you measure how well (or not) you're meeting customer expectations. You might even incorporate into that your own service standards (time) to compare to the customer's perception of the time they spent. Use GREEN sticky notes for this.

Lines and Arrows

The next step in the workshop is to add lines and arrows that designate flow and direction of interactions, exchange of value, and who controls or owns that flow and the exchanges of value. These arrows may be directional or bidirectional. Don't be shy; the point here is to identify the workflows and exchanges of value.

Dots

The last step in creating your service blueprint is to add the dots. As noted in Chapter 22, the red and green dots can be pulled from the journey map to highlight service areas that are pain points or high points for customers, especially those that are moments of truth.

The blue and purple dots will come from internal feedback, from employees and stakeholders who feel pain at a particular step or understand the root causes of customer pain. Add blue dots to those areas where you see potential cost savings or other efficiencies. Place purple dots on those areas that identify root causes of issues that need to be evaluated.

You might find that your group wants to add more dots/other colors to bring in more details in order to identify what's working and what's broken, how to prioritize (cost, resources, etc. data), areas to investigate in more detail, and more. Whatever information you need to help you make the right decisions moving forward, add it.

Now What?

You've identified tactical fixes that you can go implement now, and you've found areas that will need a major overhaul. Make those tactical fixes, then move on to develop a future-state service blueprint for how the service will be delivered in the future. (More details on this at the end of the next chapter.)

Understanding is an art, and not everyone is an artist. – Unknown

30 FUTURE-STATE MAPPING WORKSHOP

You know what the current state of the experience is and have made some tactical improvements; you've mapped what's happening under the hood to fix some immediate service delivery issues, and now, it's time to redesign the experience for the future: it's time to run a future-state journey mapping workshop.

You'll find that this chapter will be a bit abbreviated compared to the current-state mapping workshop because, where appropriate, I'll reference some of the things that you did then that you can apply now. For example, workshop supplies: you're going to need the same supplies.

As with the current-state workshops, you're going to need to define your goals, objectives, personas, and scope of the map. The scope will be defined by a current-state journey map in which you uncovered painful parts or portions of an experience that need to be completely redesigned, or you discovered that the entire experience needs to be overhauled.

Either way, you'll want to have the current-state map on the walls of your workshop site so that you can reference it. Start with a recap of why this is being redesigned, what some of the learnings were during the current-state workshop, and other details to provide context and perspective. Customers will appreciate a bit of context, which will guide and remind them to also solve for steps they may not have considered. It helps to tie it all together.

You know for which personas you're mapping, so you've got to recruit relevant customer participants. Perhaps you've arranged to have the same group back that mapped the current-state experience (or you're doing a double workshop, where half the day is focused on the current state and the other half is spent on future-state mapping), or you can start from scratch and recruit a whole new set of customers who fit the persona for whom you're redesigning the experience. (Keep in mind that the same incentive rules apply here as they did for the current-state workshop.)

As for stakeholder participants, you'll again want to make sure that the appropriate and relevant stakeholders attend the workshop. These folks must have the right level of influence to be able to take what they learn and make it happen. They've also got to be realistic about what can and can't be done.

I don't typically conduct a pre-workshop prep meeting. Instead, I'll share enough details during the recruiting call so that all participants come to the workshop knowing the task at hand. The agenda will look similar to, but likely be expanded a bit from, the example agendas posed in Chapter 25. (Again, don't short-change your time for future-state mapping if you're current-state mapping in the first half of the workshop.) Start by sharing the rules of engagement, expectations for the workshop, and an overview of what you're trying to accomplish as you open the workshop.

After introductions, ground rules, and an overview of the workshop, move into the ideation session. You've chosen your ideation approach, and you know how to conduct that type of ideation session. Remember that ideation is all about quantity of ideas over quality. Here are some quick guidelines for ideation:

- Ideation is facilitated by you; don't just think that the group can go and do this on their own.
- You must start by clearly defining the problem you are trying to solve, the problem you want customers to solve.
- Use *"How might we . . . ?"* questions to reframe the problem,

to get the ideas flowing, and to keep the answers meaningful and relevant.

- Depending on the ideation approach you use will dictate what you do next, i.e., people can call out ideas, or they can write them down first.
- I like to have them first do some independent thinking and jot their ideas on sticky notes.
- Remind them that the goal is quantity over quality.
- I also remind them to think outside the box, to think about possibilities! Rainbows and unicorns! Wild ideas! No idea is too crazy!
  - o I do remind participants that not every idea can be executed, but we take all ideas to help our internal folks develop the right solution; they may take a completely crazy idea and either learn from it or modify it to something that's doable.
- Once they've written down their ideas, go around the room, call on participants to share their ideas, and then ask them to put their sticky notes up on the designated area on the wall.
- I also remind participants that wild ideas are awesome, but being judgmental about others' ideas is not.
- They can build on others' ideas using "*Yes, and . . .*," not with "*But . . .*"
- I find myself having to remind folks to stay on topic. Be sure to do this; otherwise, you'll see how quickly and easily the conversation will stray or digress.

You will also quickly see that ideation is fun—at least, I think so!

And trust me, customers don't typically come up with outlandish ideas. Most of the things they bring up will have you scratching your head and asking, "*Yeah, why don't we do that?!*"

So what's next?

This first step that you just completed was **idea generation**. The next step is to **group the ideas**. Take the ideas and place them into common themes. You can group the ones that are saying the same thing; you can eliminate ideas that just don't make sense or don't seem to be a good fit, as deemed by the group; or you can expand and clarify ideas to figure out where they belong. The final step is to then **review the ideas** and have customers vote and prioritize them. The goal is to identify the nuggets that thread through various groups or that stand out as best next steps. This last step will feed into the future-state journey mapping process.

With that ideation session, you've primed customers for the problem they are solving and the experience they are redesigning. It's time to get up and map the future state. They've thrown out some great ideas, and they've all been captured, prioritized, and voted on. Let's see how they put it all together to design the new experience.

As facilitator, you'll want to set the stage for what you expect customers to do now. Basically, they've got to take their winning idea and put it into a timeline, into a step-by-step experience that they want to see and that your company can deliver going forward. You'll probably need to prompt them and help them get started. You might even need to take them back to the current-state map to familiarize them with how things are now—and then remind them of their ideas and how they want things to be going forward. Work with them to get started and then let them go and do the work.

What does that mean? They'll be mapping many of the same swim lanes that they mapped in the current-state map. You can use the same sticky note colors for the future-state map, to keep it simple. Here's what you'll need them to capture:

- What the customer is doing in the future to get this job done, to achieve this task
- The new future timeline for each step
- Which channels the customer will be using
- What the goals are at each step
- How the customer is feeling about each step in the journey
- Any people, tools, systems, or documents the customer will use or encounter along the way

Make sure that they spell out the experience at the same level of detail that was used for current-state mapping. Include handoffs, transitions, and things that are outside of the brand's control.

Also customers may be better able to communicate their ideas/ideals—or they may want to supplement the future-state maps—with drawings, prototypes, and other artifacts that they create during the workshop to help bring the future experience to life. This is awesome. I would actually encourage this activity!

Ultimately, what you want to see and understand from customers is: What is the ideal experience for you? How do you define ideal? How does it make you feel? What is the experience that will keep you coming back for more? What is the experience that will have you referring our brand to your friends and family?

Once customers are done mapping, the rest of the workshop is about readouts and Q&A. Have the customers designate someone to tell the story of the future experience. What are the steps? What are your goals at each step? How will you achieve (e.g., channel, etc.)? How will each step make you feel? At the end of this new journey, will you tell others about this experience?

After you hear the story from the customer's perspective, stakeholders can ask questions and get clarification to ensure they understand what the new experience should look like and the emotions it is meant to elicit.

End the workshop by thanking customers for their participation and reminding them that their ideas were heard and that you will go back, discuss, prioritize, and figure out what is feasible for the organization. Either way, close the loop with the workshop participants.

Your immediate next steps are outlined in Chapter 28; revisit that chapter. Just know that the same steps apply after future-state mapping. You've got to debrief with your stakeholders, discuss what you heard and learned, delve into feasibility of some of the ideas proposed during the workshop and consider how they might be applied, and review the future-state map. What does that mean for you? How will you implement? Can you implement? If not, why not? If not, how then? Who else needs to review and assess? Where do we go from here? What are the next steps?

***

The next thing you've got to do after all of that is settled is to develop your future-state service blueprint in order to define the onstage, backstage, and behind the scenes people, tools, systems, and processes needed for the new experience. Future-state service blueprint workshops are used to reinvent a portion of a journey that is broken or to redesign an entire journey/experience.

I won't devote a whole chapter to the future-state service blueprint workshop; instead, I'll outline a quick recap of what that looks like, with a lot of similarities to the current-state service blueprint workshop.

For the future-state service blueprint workshop, you'll:

- Have the same people in the room as you did in the current-state service blueprint workshop (stakeholders, owners, subject-matter experts).
- Hang the future-state map on the wall for reference.
- Copy the future-state journey map's DOING steps onto the service blueprint paper, as well as the channels and the onstage people, tools, and systems they interacted with.
- Ideate service delivery approaches that are different and better than what's being done today—and that will allow you to deliver the ideal experience customers designed in the future-state journey mapping workshop.
- In this workshop, you'll be designing both the onstage people, tools, systems, and documents, as well as the backstage people, tools, systems, policies, and processes.
- Plot each of these items on the blueprint to correspond with how service will be delivered for the customer in the future.
- Add the lines and arrows to show flow and direction of interactions, exchange of value, and the control of the flow and exchange.

One of the things you'll do in this workshop is capture questions that you'll need to answer, risks that you'll need to address or solve for, and anything else that requires a bit more research to ensure that you can deliver on this new blueprint. After the workshop, evaluate each of these items for feasibility or for additional details so that you and your team can feel confident in implementing this blueprint and delivering the ideal experience for your customers.

And then, you've got to implement. Refer to Chapter 24, Step Six: Implement. Develop a prototype. Test it with customers. Fail fast. Test again. Take it live. Train employees, and close the loop with customers.

. . . everything has a past. Everything—a person, an object, a word, everything. If you don't know the past, you can't understand the present and plan properly for the future. –Chaim Potok, Davita's Harp

PARTING ~~GIFTS~~ THOUGHTS

31 NOTHING CHANGES IF NOTHING CHANGES

Here we are. It's Chapter 31, and I've written about a lot of stuff. And this "stuff" is a lot of work, a lot of hard work.

It takes the entire organization to be committed to it, to work together toward a common goal, to put the "customer" in *customer* experience. You know that there's a lot of lip service about customer experience and improving the customer experience, but until you put the customer into everything you do, well, it's just that—lip service.

You can't just rebrand or paint the walls or throw technology at a people problem. No. You've got to listen to, and understand, your customers, and then you've got to use what you learn to design and deliver a better experience.

You've got to get to work.

A lot of this customer experience transformation work begins with and is really a mindset shift, which I wrote about in Chapter 4. Executives and employees alike must choose to prioritize customers and the customer experience differently; it needs to be a primary focus. Listening to customers, researching them and developing personas, and co-creating through journey mapping will help to make that shift.

Anything you can do to educate the organization about customers and the customer experience or to keep customers, their needs, and their pain points front-and-center is going to make a big difference in that mindset shift. That mindset shift ultimately needs to lead to a behavior shift as well.

I like to remind my clients that nothing changes if nothing changes. You can do everything that I've outlined in this book, but if you don't implement what you've learned, well, things just stay as they are.

You've probably seen the Dilbert cartoon where Dilbert's boss says: *"Our highest priority is satisfying our customers . . . except when it is hard . . . or unprofitable . . . or we're busy."* Don't make excuses! Make the customer experience your highest priority. (Oh, and put your employees and their experience even higher.)

Customer understanding is the cornerstone of customer-centricity. It is also a catalyst for change.

Use it to make changes! Or as General Eric Shinseki said: *"If you don't like change, you're going to like irrelevance even less."*

Put the customer in customer experience. Intentionally design the experience they desire and deserve. And watch the business achieve the intentional outcomes: growth and profitability.

Expecting things to change without putting in any effort is like waiting for a ship at the airport. – Unknown

32 AN OPEN LETTER TO CEOS

If that softer message in the last chapter didn't work, let's try this one! This is an open letter—a plea of sorts—to all CEOs that it's all about customers. Feel free to share it with your CEO!

Dear CEO:

There's a lot of talk out there about customer experience transformations stalling, or worse, failing. And there's a lot of speculation as to why that's happening. It makes no sense, but there must be an issue at the top of the organization for this to happen.

The biggest buzzword that customer experience professionals must endure today is ROI. When I've polled them at various meetings and events about what they need the most help with, they cite ROI most often. And yet, it's also the thing that is most nebulous and difficult to define. It's not like a marketing campaign, where you can just count clicks and conversion rates. A customer experience improvement initiative often takes a long time to implement and to be experienced, and there's a lot that goes into any change (people, technology, processes, enterprise-wide). Perhaps that's why it's so scary for you?

But here's the thing: why must customer experience professionals show the ROI of initiatives that will improve the customer experience? Why must they prove the business case for not pissing off customers? Why aren't these improvements and changes considered the price of doing business? Or simply how we do business? They're not about adding more work to anyone's plate; they're more about doing things better, more efficiently, and in such a way that ensures customers will come back. They're about your customers!

What's that? You're in an industry where customers have little choice or are locked into contracts for a long period of time? That's no excuse to treat customers poorly or to gouge them for services without providing any real value. Here's what's going to happen: the moment they have an opportunity (e.g., whether they move or something in their lives changes or a disruptive new start-up in your industry picks off even just a portion of the services you offer and simplifies that with a better experience that isn't harnessed by legacy technology) to move on, they will.

Here's an uncomfortable—yet indisputable—truth: you are in business to create and to nurture customers. Without customers— and especially without employees to create your products and to serve your customers—you have no business. Regardless of company size, region, industry, etc., you are in business for the customer, because of the customer.

You have "competing priorities?" What does that mean? What are those competing priorities? What could possibly compete with the foundation or the purpose of your business? What business initiative could you be considering that doesn't impact the customer?

All of those projects and initiatives and innovations happening in your organization? If you don't bring the customer voice into them, if you don't consider the impact on the customer, what's it all for?

Stop thinking that because you gained thousands of customers last month that you're delivering a great experience. You're not. Your customers don't agree. According to Bain's "delivery gap" and the reasons for the gap, you're wrong. When you focus on acquisition but not on retention, you create a leaky bucket situation that belies your truth. When you focus on moving the metric but not on improving the experience, the numbers lie.

Finding a balance between all of this really comes down to one thing: the customer. If you're focused on growth, then invest more heavily in the customer experience during the acquisition stage (yes, the experience begins well before someone becomes a customer) but not to the detriment of existing customers. If you're focused on retention, then place a disproportionate investment on improving the experience in order to retain customers.

When I hear questions like: *"But if I focus on the customer, won't that take away from my focus on the product?"* it infuriates me. Don't your employees consider that if they don't focus on the customer, then for whom are they creating the product? Where does this mindset come from? (Answer: you)

And similarly, stop trying to find a customer for your product. Find a product for your customer. I've heard this from several start-ups over the last few months. *"We have a product, but we're still trying to figure out what problem we're solving for customers."* If you're not solving problems for customers, you've got a bigger problem! Take the time to listen to—and understand—your customers. What are their needs, pain points, problems to solve, or jobs to be done? Only then can you "find a product for your customer."

Have you ever heard the story of *What the Hell is Water?* It goes like this:

> There are two young fish swimming in the ocean, and they happen to meet an older fish swimming the other way, who says, *"Morning, boys. How's the water?"* The two young fish swim on for a bit, and eventually, one of them looks at the other and says, *"What the hell is water?"*

This is a great analogy for what must happen with customers and customer experience in your organization. They must become like the water, i.e., they just are. The customer and her experience are so ingrained in your company's DNA that they just become your new normal, how you do business every day. (It should already be this way, but clearly, it's not.) Customer experience professionals are no longer selling the concepts of customer experience and customer-centricity; they're no longer building the business case and proving ROI. They don't have to. It's just what you do. It's how you do business. For and because of the customer.

In order for the business to become customer-centric, there must be a commitment from you to deliberately design the culture to put the customer at the center of all you do. What that means is that you make no decisions without asking: *"How will this impact the customer? How will this make her feel? Will this help her solve her problem?"*

I've got news for you, and it's really the bottom line: **It's all about the customer**! It's all for the customer. Everything you do. Everything you create. Every process. Every product or service. If you don't infuse the customer into your business and into everything you do, then I don't know why you're in business. It's not to maximize shareholder value. That's an outcome. But the means to get there is to relentlessly focus on the customer, day in and day out. When a great experience with your company becomes the customer's new normal, everyone, including your shareholders, will be happy.

If you need a little reality check, pause for a moment and imagine your business with no customers.

I rest my case.

Love,

Annette

Just because you don't understand it doesn't mean it isn't so. – Lemony Snicket

33 TOOLS AND CHECKLISTS

Let's be honest. You came to this last section of the book for the gifts. There aren't really any gifts, but I will provide you with some whitepapers, tools, templates, and checklists to help you as you go on this journey.

Of course, you won't get these items in this book, but once the Book page goes live on the CX Journey Inc. website (https://cx-journey.com/book), you'll find everything there, including:

- 6 Steps from Maps to Outcomes Checklist
- 30+ Reason to Map Customer Journeys Whitepaper
- The Building Blocks of a Customer Experience Transformation
- Larger versions of the graphics in this book, including
  - Action Planning Template
  - Communication Plan
  - Empathy Map Template
  - The Backbone of CEM
  - Journey Mapping Template
  - Service Blueprint Template
- Links to other journey mapping content on my website

If you have any questions about any of the content or if you can't find something, please contact me through my site.

Thank you for purchasing or borrowing this book and for reading it. If I can help you in any way, just let me know.

100% of customers are people. 100% of employees are people. If you don't understand people, you don't understand business. -Simon Sinek

ABOUT THE AUTHOR

Annette Franz, CCXP is founder and Chief Experience Officer of CX Journey Inc. She's got more than 25 years of experience in both helping companies understand their employees and customers and identify what drives retention, satisfaction, engagement, and the overall experience. She has worked with both B2B and B2C brands in a multitude of industries.

Annette was named one of "The 100 Most Influential Tech Women on Twitter" by *Business Insider* and is an internationally-recognized customer experience thought leader, influencer, speaker, and author.

She serves as Vice Chairwoman on the Board of Directors of the Customer Experience Professionals Association (CXPA), mentors other professionals in this field to help them advance their careers, and is a speaker and an avid writer; you can find her thought leadership not only on her own site (https://cx-journey.com) but also in *Forbes*, Business2Community, CustomerThink, Quality Digest, *APICS Magazine*, and more. She is CEM Certified and is a Certified Customer Experience Professional (CCXP).

She is also an official member of the Forbes Coaches Council, an invitation-only community for successful business and career coaches. Members are selected based on their depth and diversity of experience.

And finally, she is an Advisory Board Member for CX@Rutgers.

There is a great difference between knowing and understanding: you can know a lot about something and not really understand it. - Charles F. Kettering

Made in the USA
Monee, IL
12 March 2022

92758237R00125